For Sharo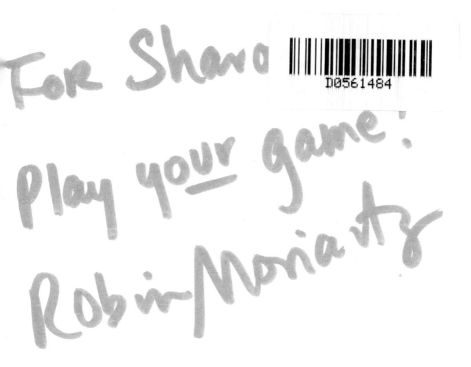
Play you*r* game!
Robin Moriarty

Advance Praise

"This book is perfect for anyone seeking to take control of how they play the game at work. Its honest and accessible approach will guide you to achieve the success that you desire!"

—GAIL EVANS, former EVP, CNN Newsgroup and author of *Play Like a Man, Win Like a Woman*

"Compelling, refreshing, honest, and inspiring. *What Game Are You Playing?* reminds us that it's never too late to design your own life game, fearlessly act on it, and actually enjoy playing it!"

—ERIKA MEDINA-VECCHINI, Managing Director, Endeavor Puerto Rico

"Are you grinding through life? Then hit the reset button, and wipe your slate clean! This book helps you redefine success so that you can pursue what is important to you. Stop trying to live up to others' expectations, and start playing your game, by your rules, today!"

—DON W. QUIGLEY JR., retired Fortune 100 President

"As an entrepreneur, I know that work is a huge part of life. This book helps you figure out how to insure that *your* life and *your* work are fulfilling *your* needs. It is a must-read for young people entering the workforce and for moms going back to work!"

—SHAYNE WALSEY, President, Urban Enterprises

"This is a guidebook for the dreamers, the artists, the hustlers, and the individuals. The people who have realized their lives are theirs to live and the people who want to find that realization. In other words, this is for all of us."

—JEREMY PETRANKA, PhD, Assistant Dean and Associate Professor of the Practice, The Fuqua School of Business at Duke University

A FRAMEWORK FOR REDEFINING SUCCESS AND
ACHIEVING WHAT MATTERS MOST

WHAT GAME

Are You

PLAYING?

ROBIN MORIARTY, PhD

GREENLEAF
BOOK GROUP PRESS

This publication is designed to provide accurate and authoritative information in regard to the subject matter covered. It is sold with the understanding that the publisher and author are not engaged in rendering legal, accounting, or other professional services. Nothing herein shall create an attorney-client relationship, and nothing herein shall constitute legal advice or a solicitation to offer legal advice. If legal advice or other expert assistance is required, the services of a competent professional should be sought.

Published by Greenleaf Book Group Press
Austin, Texas
www.gbgpress.com

Copyright ©2019 Happy Happy LLC

Distributed by Greenleaf Book Group

For ordering information or special discounts for bulk purchases, please contact Greenleaf Book Group at PO Box 91869, Austin, TX 78709, 512.891.6100.

Design and composition by Greenleaf Book Group and Kim Lance
Cover design by Greenleaf Book Group and Kim Lance
Cover Illustration: Copyright by Reinekke, 2019. Used under license from Shutterstock.com

Publisher's Cataloging-in-Publication data is available.

Print ISBN: 978-1-62634-653-6

eBook ISBN: 978-1-62634-654-3

Part of the Tree Neutral® program, which offsets the number of trees consumed in the production and printing of this book by taking proactive steps, such as planting trees in direct proportion to the number of trees used: www.treeneutral.com

TreeNeutral

Printed in the United States of America on acid-free paper

19 20 21 22 23 24   10 9 8 7 6 5 4 3 2 1

First Edition

Thank you to Paul for bursting into my office that day.
And to Gail Evans for her book *Play Like a Man, Win Like a Woman*, which helped me realize early on that this is all just a big game anyway.

Table of Contents

What Game Are You Playing?

One November afternoon, I was in my office, sitting in the chair behind my desk, drinking a cup of coffee, and typing away at emails on my computer.

I was pretty relaxed and plugging along at my work when all of a sudden, one of my favorite colleagues burst into the room. He was noticeably ticked off about something. Because he's a pretty big person, he really filled up the space in the office and was huffing and puffing and pacing back and forth and waving his arms around.

In between huffs and puffs, he let on that he was upset because our CEO's new compensation package had just been announced and . . . well . . . let's just say that our CEO was earning significantly more than either one of us. And my colleague was furious.

He said, "He's winning! *That* guy! He's winning! And we're *losing!*"

I looked up from my computer, smiled at him, and replied matter-of-factly, "Well, I don't know what you're talking about because *I'm winning.*"

He stopped dead in his tracks and turned to me with con-fusion on his face—like, "How could you be winning? I know you're not making as much money as our CEO!"

So I continued, "I'm playing the game of 'Spending the Most Amount of Time in the Coolest Places.' And I'm winning!" And I proudly pointed to a huge calendar hanging on my wall. You know those calendars. You can see all 12 months of the year at once, and you can write on them with dry-erase markers in different colors. On the calendar, in large blue, orange, pink, and purple letters, I had written all the places I had gone over the course of the year for work and for play.

With a look that was somewhere between bewilderment and skepticism, he turned and looked at my calendar. He saw that I had been to Berlin and London and Hong Kong and Buenos

Aires and Sydney and Shanghai and Toronto and a few other places over the course of the year.

And he paused to consider. He knew I was losing the game of "Who Makes the Most Money in the Company." But he also knew that I was definitely winning the "Spending the Most Time in the Coolest Places" game.

I told him that there was more than one game to play and that maybe he needed to think about which game he was choosing to play. I reminded him that it's important to play your *own* game—not the game that other people are playing or the game that they want you to play, but the game that *you* want to play. And I reminded him that it's more important to win at your *own* game than to try to win at someone else's. And he said that I was brilliant and that I should write a book about it.

So for Paul, here it is.

And for everybody else, I ask: What game are you playing?

Redefining Success

As long as I can remember, I have felt the weight of others' expectations on me—about how I should behave, choices I should make, and what being successful should look like. I believed all I had been taught about what I should seek in my life—degrees from prestigious universities, a high-powered career, promotions and impressive titles, a big house in the best neighborhood, a brilliant spouse, children who are super smart and natural athletes, fancy cars, a stylish wardrobe, a fit body with six-pack abs, a face without wrinkles, good hair, white teeth, a healthy glow (but not from too much sun), luxury watches and accessories, vacations to wine country, early retirement, keeping up with the Joneses (or better yet, beating them), and ultimately, external applause and admiration from neighbors, colleagues, friends, and followers.

I absorbed those messages and curated my life so that I would meet others' expectations both at work and at home, and I tried to live what I had been taught to think of as a successful life. I compared myself to others and often felt like a loser, especially when it seemed like others were doing better than I was. And social media made it worse because someone is *always* doing better—with a bigger house, a better body, a more exotic vacation.

⊙ ⊙ ⊙

After pushing myself hard to pursue the version of success that had been defined for me by others, I realized that comparing myself to the people around me and living my life by others' rules was exhausting, frustrating, and causing a great deal of anxiety. It was not fulfilling, I was not experiencing any internal calm, and, quite frankly, I was kind of dying inside from the grind.

I wanted to make changes, but it was really difficult, and I had no idea how to start. I read books that encouraged me to set and track goals, to get a job doing my passion, and to go on a holiday to beat the burnout. These books were telling me that by setting and tracking goals, I would get the next big job and achieve financial success. They were guiding me to start a company based on my passion and promising that financial rewards and external accolades would follow. One even encouraged me to take a vacation, because upon return I'd be so productive that surely I'd get a promotion and more money. Basically, these books were nudging me in a direction consistent with the version of success that had been defined for me by others; but I had a nagging feeling this definition of success was the problem in the first place. They were promising that I could *have it all*, yet I kept thinking, *Why would I*

Why would I want it all? Why wouldn't I just want what I want and not what everyone else says I should want?

want it all? Why wouldn't I just want what I want and not what everyone else says I should want?

So I sought out other kinds of books that had wildly different perspectives. Some of them encouraged me to do things like go off the grid, abandon material goods, or move to an ashram. As appealing as those options sounded, especially in the midst of burnout, they were not plausible choices for me as I wasn't really interested in abandoning my relationships or the comforts of my material life. I was just looking for a way to enjoy them instead of being owned by them.

Also I started noticing that the books I'd read all seemed to imply that once I did whatever the author advised, everything would fall into place easily and quickly in a snap. They seemed to be saying that immediately after taking their advice, I would all of a sudden be living a perfect, happy life and I would have it all. This seemed implausible, as my life experience taught me that things rarely, if ever, happen easily and quickly. Life is hard work, and things take time.

During that phase of my life, I was in the fortunate position of being able to travel to different countries for my job. With a telecommunications company, I spent a year on a project in Tel Aviv, and I spent several years traveling 50–60 percent of the time for projects in places like Germany, Ecuador, Peru, and Brazil. I even moved to Argentina with that company, and while there, I worked with people from Chile, Uruguay, and Venezuela. Later, with a different company, I moved from Argentina to Hong Kong and had interactions with people across Asia, most notably in China, Korea, Taiwan, Vietnam, and Thailand. Over the past

few years in my work, with yet another multinational corporation, I have been living in the US and traveling to Europe, Latin
America, Canada, and Asia-Pacific. I have also had the opportunity to travel to Shanghai, Delhi, Ho Chi Minh City, Istanbul,
Prague, London, Lima, and Santiago to teach MBA students
about cross-cultural leadership.

Through these extensive international experiences, I have
come to realize that other cultures don't define success in the
same way as the US. For example, in Latin America, there
tends to be a greater focus on family and friendship than in
the US. The definition of family is broader and includes aunts,
uncles, cousins, and other extended family members. The whole
family gets together often and they are very involved in each
other's lives. The focus is on relationships and social fulfillment
more than on material financial success. In Asia, the famous
filial piety of Chinese cultures is real, as is respect for elders in
Japan and Korea, which is in stark comparison to the worship-
ing of youth in the US. In Mediterranean cultures and their
diaspora, there is more focus on enjoyment of weekends and
holidays—with work emails turned off—and food, wine, and
social activities deeply ingrained in daily life. In those cultures,
you are definitely not seen as successful if you are grinding away
on work emails on nights and weekends, in contrast to the US.
In the Middle Eastern cultures with which I'm familiar, there's
more focus on living in the present, compared to the US where
we're instructed to plan and save for our futures.

•   ◉   ●

Once I realized there was more than one way to define a successful life, I started trying out other definitions of success. This helped me realize how constrained our definitions are in the US, particularly with the focus on financial success and on competing and winning, which inevitably forces you to compare yourself to others, which feels unhealthy. I started letting go of comparisons with others and revamped my daily activities around new definitions of success. I turned off work emails on holidays and weekends, I intentionally went out more in the evenings with friends instead of going to bed early to be fresh for work the next day, and I let myself sleep in guilt-free when I was tired.

Instead of measuring how many hours I'd clocked at work or how much money was in my bank account, I started measuring my new experiences: classes I was taking; new restaurants and neighborhoods I was visiting; and events and shows I was exposing myself to. In this process, I found that seeking types of success that were related to gaining new experiences, learning new languages and cultures, and sharing what I'd learned with others were a thousand times

I discovered that I was healthier and happier using other measures of success rather than the ones that I had been raised to pursue.

more fulfilling for me than pursuing a promotion or a larger paycheck. I discovered that I was healthier and happier using other measures of success rather than the ones that I had been raised to pursue.

● ● ●

Even though I knew I was healthier, happier, and felt quite successful based on my new measures, I was struck by how difficult it was to shift my behavior in order to chase other types of success that were new for me. After all, I had been trained to think of success and what I should be doing in a certain way. I had been trained to be competitive and success-oriented based on the US definition of success, and I needed to feel like I was winning, even after I'd redefined success for myself based on decidedly non-quantifiable measures.

I noticed that this was difficult, too, because when I made changes to my life and the way I lived, I felt I was being judged by others. And if I'm honest, I was judging myself too, for not working hard enough or for no longer choosing work over fun. I was told it was a phase. I was told I was being foolish and selfish and worse. I was told I wasn't reaching my full potential because I wasn't following the traditional model of success. And I was told those things by people who were close to me, which didn't feel very good.

Since I'm a learner at heart, I wanted to understand why it was so difficult for me to embrace a new definition of success and make big changes in my life even when I knew that those changes were making me healthier and happier. After all, I'd read the books that said I should just stop caring about what other people think. But the truth is, I did care! They said once I stopped caring about what others think, everything would magically become great and perfect. But something was getting in the way for me.

● ● ●

I decided to take my research a little further. I picked up a book on cultural conditioning called *Cultures and Organizations: Software of the Mind*; psychology magazines like *Psychology Today*, *Science Direct*, and *Scientific American Mind*; and books about how your brain works like *The Body Keeps the Score* and *Rewire Your Anxious Brain*. This material was fascinating, and I learned that we are conditioned about what is right and wrong by our parents, teachers, communities, and societies and that this conditioning implicitly includes pursuing a certain definition of success. I also learned that our brains are wired to do things that others expect of us and that our brains get uncomfortable and have little freak-outs when others aren't happy with us. Through this research, I realized that one of the reasons making changes was so difficult was because not only was *my* brain freaking out by doing something outside what I'd been taught to do, but *other* people's brains were also freaking out when they saw me doing something that they didn't expect me to do.

I realized that one of the reasons making changes was so difficult was because not only was *my* brain freaking out by doing something outside what I'd been taught to do, but *other* people's brains were also freaking out when they saw me doing something that they didn't expect me to do.

Essentially, through the process of conditioning, we're trained to want certain things, behave in certain ways, and avoid ostracizing ourselves from support groups for survival's sake. So when you start trying to do something different, both you and others around you feel uncomfortable and struggle; in many ways, that discomfort is what pulls you back to the status quo. It's what pulls us back to acting "normal," and it's what keeps us doing what is expected instead of branching out to do something different.

◦ ◦ ◦

Once I figured that out, I started thinking about redefining success and changing my behavior from another direction, and it seemed less daunting. Instead of expecting a moment where everything would magically be perfect, I realized that with some effort and awareness, I could move past my conditioned behavior and pursue success in different ways while also managing those around me differently if they responded negatively to changes I was making in my life. I could help them understand *why* I was changing and give them a little warning so it wouldn't be such a shock. Through this realization, I became more thoughtful about seeking support from different kinds of people, and I came up with some worksheets and checklists along the way that helped me think through those changes.

◦ ◦ ◦

Through this process, things unfolded for me. I have been able to redefine success and redesign my life in a way that doesn't feel like a grind and where I honestly, deep in my heart, no longer compare myself to others or feel like a loser. In fact, I feel like more of a winner than I ever have, even though so many elements of that traditional US definition of success are absent from my life. I feel like a winner because I define success in a way that works for me and leads me to pursue the things that are important to me—rather than the things that others have told me should be important to me. It's a fundamental, huge difference in the way I think.

Now, this is not to say that my life is always perfect or that everything is always great. Things go up and down, like health and work and friendships and relationships. This is normal and just a part of life. But because I'm focused on my own definition of success and not wasting energy on things that are important to other people, I can manage the challenges that arise. I no longer carry around the burden of others' expectations.

After the serendipitous inter-action with a work colleague mentioned in the Preface, I was encouraged to share these perspec-tives with others. Apparently I'm not the only one who has been stressed out over comparing myself to others. I'm not the only one who has felt like a failure for not meeting others' expecta-tions. And I'm not the only one asking myself what am I doing with my life. Apparently, there are a lot of us who want to feel good about our choices, who want to redefine success for our-selves, and who want tools to create more fulfillment and valida-tion regarding our life choices at work and at home.

> **Because I'm focused on my own definition of success and not wasting energy on things that are important to other people, I can manage the challenges that arise. I no longer carry around the burden of others' expectations.**

• ◦ •

In this book, you'll find what I hope you'll think is a fun and accessible approach to answering these big questions both personally and professionally. Through the worksheets, exercises, and examples, this book may help you see how you've been conditioned to define success a certain way and then help you step away from that definition so that you can define and pursue your own version of success. The pages in this book will help you map out what you'll need to get there.

> **When you are clear about your goal and you move with consistency toward it, you will reach it. Not magically or mystically, but because of your hard work.**

Finally, I recognize that answering big questions about your personal and professional life and then making changes accordingly is not easy. It takes courage, support, and strength. This book also will help you figure out how to find that so you feel emboldened as you define and pursue your own path. After all, when you are clear about your goal and you move with consistency toward it, you will reach it. Not magically or mystically, but because of your hard work. Because *you* make it happen.

I'll admit that learning something and then sharing what I've learned with others brings me great joy, so the motivation for this book is partly selfish. But mostly my hope is that by sharing what I've learned, you won't spend as many years as I did trying to figure this stuff out. You'll move toward a new definition of success and a healthier and happier mind-set more quickly than I did. So let's get started!

CHAPTER 1

It's All a Game,
and Everybody Is Playing

E arly in my career, I had the good fortune to be given a book by my boss. The book was written by Gail Evans, the first female senior leader at CNN and a general badass. The book, *Play Like a Man, Win Like a Woman*, is a sort of guidebook for women working in large corporations. Its core argument is that women tend to be disadvantaged in corporate America because there's a game going on that the guys seem to get intuitively but that the women seem to miss. Specifically, men seem to understand better than women that the object of the game is to get the biggest title and the most money and that you do that by choosing your team, getting more resources, delivering results, tooting your horn, advocating for what you want, and playing your cards right.

Gail writes, "Whether the game is croquet, Monopoly, field hockey, or football, you have to understand the directions first. So why play the game of business any differently? Business is as much a game as any other board, individual, or team sports game."[1] Realizing this was life changing for me. After I read

---

1 Gail Evans, *Play Like a Man, Win Like a Woman* (New York: Crown Business, 2001), 6–7.

this book, I started noticing the games people were playing at work. I also noticed all of the indicators that you are winning the game at work—the size of your office, the number of people reporting to you, and the size of the budgets you manage, to name a few.

And I noticed the ways different people played the game: by tooting their own horn, by stabbing others in the back, or by innovating and creating new solutions. You may have seen this as well, with colleagues who have sucked up to their superiors to get promoted or who have taken credit for the work of others. You may have seen those who manipulate information and perceptions to get more resources in their group so that they can feel more powerful. Unfortunately, you may have even known colleagues who have launched campaigns to tear another person down—by diminishing or ostracizing or gossiping about them—all in an effort to make themselves look better.

Some people play the game by trying to become indispensable at work. In an effort to create job security for themselves, they hoard information, hire mediocre team members, and work to convince the organization that they are irreplaceable. I think those people are actually playing the game wrong, because if you manage a team of underperformers, you're unlikely to achieve your objectives—and therefore you become disposable. Others take a different approach. They hire great people and then create, innovate, and maybe even get to go home early because their team has everything under control, which seems like a much better way to play the game, if you ask me.

In her book, Gail Evans goes on to say, "For me, the object of the game is simply to feel great about what you do. That's the most important objective of all—because that's how you end up feeling fulfilled, and that's how you win. I know for a fact that I have been successful because I've always loved my jobs."[2] Gail is the one who taught me that my work life is a game, and she played her own game, which was to feel great about what she does. And she's still living her life by that definition of success today.

The Bigger Game Is Life

Reading Gail's book and shifting my thinking about my professional life helped me realize that it's not just work that is a game, but life as well. The problem is that in life, as in work, most of us don't realize there's a game going on. Most of us don't see the rules of the game that we've been conditioned to play. At work, you may recognize that the objective is to be the CEO and make the most money, and you can make moves toward that objective.

You can do that in life too. But most of us aren't explicit about the objectives of our life games. We don't even see that there's a larger game going on. If you have a choice about how you're going to play the game at work, don't you also have the ability to choose how you'll play the game of life? And can't you design the game instead of just playing the one handed to you? So what if you start thinking of not just work as a game but your broader life as well?

2 Evans, *Play Like a Man, Win Like a Woman*, 13.

Play by Your Own Rules

Just as you know people who are playing games at work, you may also know people who seem to be playing their life game by their own rules. They may be the people who work from 7 a.m. to 3 p.m. so they can coach their kid's soccer team in the afternoon, or perfect their rock band's new set, or train for the Olympics, or care for a family member in need. They may also be the people who are working primarily for healthcare and other benefits because their partner is starting a small business or because they are attending night school. They may be people who forego promotions to maintain flexible hours and avoid the headaches that can come with managing people. Or they may be people like me, actively seeking assignments that involve travel and adventure.

To help bring clarity to these ideas, let me tell you about one of my friends. He chose a career as a teacher to middle schoolers. He did not choose this because he loves adolescents and the interesting situations that adolescents get themselves into when he chaperones them on overnight school field trips. He chose this because he loves workdays that end at defined times so that he has time to go to the gym before dinner. He chose this because he likes to be at the same school where his kids are during the day in case there is some type of emergency. And he chose this because he loves summers off and

People playing their own game have a level of calm, a level of clarity, and a level of contentment that's lacking in those who are getting played as pawns in someone else's game.

the unstructured time for his hobbies and his family. He also chose to marry someone who owns her own business. They both are great at what they do and enjoy their work; but instead of putting financial objectives ahead of everything else, they've put flexibility and time for the kids at the forefront of their decisions. This way, if something goes wrong, they don't have to stress about who has to miss a meeting or whose boss will get mad if they leave early. They have it covered. Because they designed it that way.

These are the people who have figured out how to arrange their work to fit into their lives. They are playing their own game instead of someone else's. They have a level of calm, a level of clarity, and a level of contentment that's lacking in those who are getting played as pawns in someone else's game.

Play the Right Kind of Game

Now, some of you may be thinking that playing games is bad. You may see it as manipulative and disingenuous in terms of motives. There are certainly games that I don't encourage or condone. These are the games that are primarily concerned with tearing others down, such as when someone is sabotaging someone else or taking credit for their work. But there are games you can play to help build yourself and others up. These are games focused on learning new skills, expanding your thinking, and pulling in positivity.

Remember that we all played games as kids, and depending on what you played, you learned key skills like teamwork, critical thinking, the ability to balance short-term and long-term goals, speed, and quick-wittedness while playing those games. We can take these skills that we learned as children and apply them to our lives as adults.

Seeing your life as a bigger game—and realizing that you can define the rules and play it consciously—can help you focus, pause, and distance yourself so that you can see the big picture, see choices that you can make, and make the choices that will help you get to where you want to be.

And where is it that you really want to be?

> **Seeing your life as a bigger game–and realizing that you can play it consciously–can help you focus, pause, and distance yourself so that you can see the big picture, see choices that you can make, and make the choices that will help you get to where you want to be.**

What Do You Want?

One of the hardest things to do is figure out what you want. With school and work and friends and family and loves and fun and hobbies and everything else to consider, where do you even start?

Most people I know start filling up that blank slate that asks, "What do I want to do with my life?" with things they're supposed to want. They put in the big life blocks they've been trained to think about, like schooling and degrees, jobs and titles and career progression, meeting a life partner, having children, buying first houses then second houses, planning for kids' private schools and colleges, and retiring early with enough in the bank to never have to work again. And they attach dates and timelines to each of these activities.

This is so common that I never even gave it a thought until one evening, I was having drinks with a friend, and she was panicking and sharing that her life plan was off track. She explained that in order to have two children by a certain age, she needed to meet someone, spend two years dating him, then get married and spend at least one year married without children, and then nine months for the first baby, then a year, then nine months for the second baby, and boom! She needed to meet that special someone that very night in that very bar or else her vision for her life and the timeline she had created would be broken and she would be a failure.

I remember thinking, *Oh my dear friend, maybe your life won't go as you've planned, but maybe it will surprise you and be even better. Mine certainly has. Leave yourself open to that possibility instead of staying so focused on something that may not happen.*

Another friend shared with me the stress he was under as a 27-year-old single man. He'd amassed around $75K in debt, was living in New York in an apartment with several roommates, and was trying to find a salaried job. He enjoyed his hourly work in the sports industry, which included tickets to sporting events and regular run-ins with professional athletes. He was happy and enjoying his life, but he felt pressure to find a stable job so that he could pay off his debt, attract a partner, and buy an apartment where eventually he'd live with a spouse and children.

As we were talking, I asked him if he actually wanted to have an apartment and a spouse and children. He said he wasn't sure, but that's what he was supposed to want, and he admitted that he felt like a failure because he'd never be able to get there at this rate.

With a full slate defined, people set off on a path of pursuing the definition of success they've been taught to want.

This struck me as odd, because he was feeling like a failure for not having something he didn't even know if he wanted in the first place! He was frustrated that others his age were living with a partner and seemed to be doing better than he was financially, even though he didn't think they were having as many cool experiences or enjoying their work lives as much as he was. Although he was pretty happy with the path he was currently on, he couldn't help but feel like a failure because he was comparing himself to others who seemed further down the path of success than he was. And again, it was a path he wasn't even sure he wanted to go down.

I reminded him there were many ways to live, and in all versions he could have love and happiness and success. The key was to define the version of success that worked for him and then to go after it intentionally with gusto and without comparing himself to others.

When answering the question "What do I want to do with my life?" the slate gets filled up with things we're supposed to be doing and the vision seems full, overwhelming even, with no room for anything else. With a full slate defined, people set off on a path of pursuing the definition of success they've been taught to want. And they haven't even had the chance to think about what they really want, much less explore it.

Inevitably a few years down the road, some reflecting happens and people realize that their slate is filled with things they didn't even want in the first place. But now they have a mortgage and bills to pay and maybe a spouse or children and people to whom they've made commitments, and unwinding it all to go in a different direction seems more and more difficult.

As a result, they end up missing the joy in life. Because the plan did not include time for surf classes or to learn the guitar or to write music or to just play with the dog. The plan did not include tending to the garden or learning a language or having relationships of both the meaningful and pointless varieties. The plan did not include job shifts or new opportunities and paths through which they could grow, expand, and change. Instead, they vigorously pursue the plan and timeline they created for themselves based on the definition of success and the pursuit of things that they are supposed to want according to other people.

Additionally, in their effort to check off the boxes in their plan and timeline, often they forget to make sure their activities and relationships are actually healthy and fulfilling. I've known people who work 90 hours a week with toxic bosses and others who have intimate relationships with manipulative partners. But they tolerate and overlook these unhealthy and unfulfilling situations because they feel they need the job and the relationship so that all of the boxes in their plan and timeline are checked.

No one includes in their plan the chance encounter in an airport with a perfect stranger who perhaps changes your whole life with a few words and a new perspective. Or the way a movie can touch your soul and move you to action. Or the raucous laughter—the hoots and howls—with your friends. Or the deliciousness of

If you think of your life as a game, and especially as one that you design, you will start feeling like you have more control and more choices because you will be playing your own game by your own rules.

staying out dancing all night and watching the sun rise on your way home. We take for granted that those things will happen and that joy will occur in our lives without having to put them on our calendar.

I encourage you to wipe your slate clean for now so you can go through the exercises in this book and intentionally put in your plan things that are meaningful and relevant to you instead of things that others have encouraged you to include. After all, if you think of your life as a game, and especially as one that you design, you will start feeling like you have more control and more choices because you will be playing your own game by your own rules. When you play your own game, *you* write the rules, *you* decide what winning looks like, *you* control the choices, *you* make the moves, and *you* can design the game to be what you want it to be.

So no matter what game others are playing, you're playing your *own* game, and you're winning.

REMEMBER:

- This is all a game, so make it a game you want to play, with your *own* definition of success and the pursuit of things that are actually important to *you*.

CHAPTER 2

Are You Playing Your Own Game
or Someone Else's?

T he truth is that you are already playing a bigger life game, even though you may not realize you've been playing it. And it's probably a game you've been conditioned to play rather than a game you've chosen for yourself.

We are all conditioned (or socialized, if you prefer that word) with certain core values and beliefs, with certain cultural narratives, and with certain ideas about the way things are supposed to be. In the book *Culture and Organizations: Software of the Mind*, the authors write, "The sources of one's mental programs lie within the social environments in which one grew up and collected one's life experiences. The programming starts with the family: it continues within the neighborhood, at school, in youth groups, at the workplace, and in the living community."[1] We internalize others' ideas as our own until we gain the awareness and perspective that leads to the realization that we can choose to continue playing that game or we can choose to play a different game.

---

1 Geert Hofstede, Gert Jan Hofstede, and Michael Minkov, *Culture and Organizations: Software of the Mind* (New York: McGraw-Hill Education, 2010), 5.

We Are All Conditioned

This conditioning process is a part of every society. It includes the values that get passed down through generations, the myths that a society believes about itself and others, the principles that guide behaviors, and the definitions of what makes for a good life. This conditioning starts when you are a child, continues through your schooling, and goes on into your working years. It can be so comprehensive that you don't even know it's happening. You assume that others think like you do and that they share your perspectives—although they may not. You assume that their conditioning was the same as yours—although it may not have been. You assume because of your conditioning that there's a right way and a way things are supposed to be—although much of your society may not be reflected in that. Basically, because of this cultural conditioning, you assume everyone else is seeing the world through the same lens that you are. You assume they are playing the same game you're playing and that they understand the rules the same way that you do.

Because of cultural conditioning, you assume everyone else is seeing the world through the same lens that you are.

Conditioning isn't necessarily a bad thing. In fact, it can be quite useful for a functioning society. Imagine how many informal behaviors happen every day without anyone even thinking about them, like arriving at a street corner and looking both ways before crossing the street. If you are from the US, you are likely to look first to the left, then to the right, then to the left again before crossing the street. That's because in the US, you're most likely to get hit by traffic coming from your left, given the side of the road we drive on. In the UK, people look first to the right because that's where the traffic is coming from. Also in London, there are a lot of one-way streets, so it's not always easy to figure out which direction the traffic is coming from. As a result, I always find myself being extra cautious when crossing the street and I look both ways many times before stepping off the curb. Apparently I'm not the only one who has trouble. This is such an issue that in London, every street corner has a reminder spray-painted on the sidewalk to ensure that tourists LOOK RIGHT or LOOK LEFT toward the direction of oncoming traffic so they don't get taken out by a double-decker bus! To keep people from getting hit by a bus, it's helpful for everyone to be conditioned to look out for traffic in effective ways. Some might say it's instinct, but it's really behavior that has been conditioned so deeply that it feels like instinct, even though it's not. There's no real reason to look to the right or to the left first. It's just conditioning.

If you multiply this example a million times, you can get a sense of how much conditioning comes into your daily life in the form of things that you don't even think about. Which soap is for your hair and which is for your dishes? What behaviors are normal in your commute when cars need to merge into one lane or when people need to merge into one subway turnstile? Do you let the person next to you go first or do you cut them off? Where do vegetables get weighed in the supermarket—in the vegetable section or at the checkout? Do you stand in line to wait for the bus or get on a subway, or do you just sort of crowd around where you think the door will open? There are many examples in routine daily tasks, but conditioning goes even deeper. As Hofstede et al. explain, conditioning begins in childhood. Think about the time you spent in the classroom in grade school. You had to show up on time and be in your seat when the bell rang to start the day. If you were late, it was not a good thing. Then you'd do some schoolwork and go outside for a 20-minute recess before going back inside for more schoolwork. Around midday, you would eat lunch with classmates, then you'd return to your classroom for the final push of schoolwork before hearing the bell ring and dashing out of school as fast as possible to get on your bus or get in your car to go home.

Whenever I am in an office environment, I am struck by how much the office rhythm mimics the school rhythm because we've been conditioned for it to feel comfortable. We arrive to our desks at a designated time, sit down to plow through emails, have some meetings, take a 20-minute coffee break, and chat with coworkers. Then we return to our desks, have lunch with colleagues, and endure the final push of meetings until we can dash out the door to go home as fast as possible. Our daily agendas are scheduled in 30- or 60-minute increments, just like our classes were. If we show up too late or leave too early, it is noticed—and not necessarily in a good way, just like in grade school.

This conditioning starts in grade school and continues into college. At the university I attended, students lived in dorms and we rode buses around to different parts of the campus. My dorm room was tiny and the buses were always crowded. They were so crowded that you had to stand up and hang on to the bar at the top of the bus to keep your balance. One day when my mom was visiting and we were on the bus, she said, "You know, I think they're preparing you all to live in New York." And I think she was right. We were being educated, but we were also being trained to do certain kinds of jobs in certain kinds of urban environments.

In graduate school, the conditioning is disguised as training for certain kinds of professions. In law school, students are taught how to argue, which is helpful in the legal profession. Medical school teaches you to quickly assess situations and make critical decisions on no sleep. I'm not sure it's necessary for residencies to be so brutal with their hours, but I won't argue with the need to be able to make decisions quickly in emergency situations. Business schools are structured around team building and networking, as success in business is built on getting things done with and through others as well as on developing relationships with people in your company and industry.

In his book *Multiple Choice*, Alejandro Zambra uses an innovative way to highlight how school does not exactly teach us how to think. School teaches us how to function in a society that has a specific definition of success as well as unwritten rules regarding what we are supposed to do and how we are supposed to do it. School teaches you how to play the game you are expected to play without really exploring whether or not it's the game you want to play. Alejandro reminds us, "You weren't educated. You were trained."[2] That's conditioning.

When we analyze all the many different ways we are

---

2 Alejandro Zambra, *Multiple Choice* (London: Penguin Books, 2016), 71.

conditioned in our lives, we can see just how much we are affected by it. In order to move past this conditioning and find out what we really want to do with our lives, we must get a handle on and differentiate between what we are supposed to want and what we really want.

The Game You've Probably Been Conditioned to Play

Remember, conditioning is a part of every society, and it's not necessarily bad. It just means that someone else is defining your bigger game of life for you.

To illustrate this, I will use an example from the US: the concept of the American Dream. This is a great concept, and people from the US have been conditioned since childhood to accept the key premises of the American Dream. These premises are a fundamental part of being American, and as such, challenging them leads to a lot of negative reactions.

Something I loved about teaching was telling my MBA students that they were conditioned, having them disagree with me, and then putting up a chart with key premises of the American Dream and hearing them respond robotically as they answered out loud and in unison to fill-in-the-blanks statements like "All men are _____" and "Life, liberty, and _____." They realized they had accepted and internalized the concepts without really thinking about them.

The premises of the American Dream include the fundamental belief that you can be anything you want to be with hard work (despite the systemic challenges that make it easier for some than others), that all people are equal (despite structural inequalities), that we have the right to life, liberty, and the pursuit of happiness (and that happiness includes some level of financial success and security).

When we bring these premises down to a practical level, the American Dream gets further defined to traditionally include:

- Marriage without divorce
- Children with that spouse
- The concept of family defined as parents and their offspring
- Children leave the parents' home after finishing schooling
- Home ownership
- A stable 9–5 job with weekends off
- Two weeks of paid vacation
- A retirement where one doesn't work or live with their adult children

These ideas are reinforced structurally through the following:

- Tax deductions for home ownership
- Tax advantages for having children
- Tax incentives for retirement savings
- Eligibility requirements for a family's medical and other benefits
- Entire industries built around weddings
- Entire industries built around retirement living
- Limited and set times for school and business hours
- The higher education industry promoted as your ticket to a successful future (including student loans!)

Although in the US it is considered the norm that people will be married, have children, and live with their nuclear family, the data from surveys and the US census show that this family situation is not as common as our overarching cultural narrative would have us believe. In the US, only 44 percent of households are comprised of married people, so 56 percent of households do not involve marriage;[3] 37 percent of non-parents aged 18–49 say they don't plan to have any children;[4] 61.5 percent of 25–34-year-olds have no kids;[5] more than 10 percent of parents of kids under 18 are also caring for an older adult at the same time;[6] and 15 percent of 25–35-year-olds were living in their parents' home.[7]

---

3 Emily Schondelmeyer, "More Adults Living Without Children," United States Census Bureau, August 9, 2017.

4 Gretchen Livingston and Juliana Menasce Horowitz, "Most Parents—and Many Non-Parents—Don't Expect to Have Kids in the Future," Pew Research Center.

5 Schondelmeyer, "More Adults Living Without Children."

6 Gretchen Livingston, "More than one-in-ten US parents are also caring for an adult," Pew Research Center, November 29, 2018.

7 Richard Fry, "It's becoming more common for young adults to live at home—and for longer stretches," Pew Research Center, May 5, 2017.

Clearly the data does not match the narrative that we have been taught to aspire to, where a household is comprised of a married couple with kids under 18, where kids leave their parents' house by their early 20s, and where older generations don't live with younger ones. And deviations from these paths are seen as noteworthy because they're not what you'd expect. Just stand in a supermarket checkout line and read the headlines on the magazine rack, and you'll see articles about those "weird" deviations.

- Adult children who live at home!
- Women who choose not to have children!
- Celebrity divorces!
- People working during their retirement years!

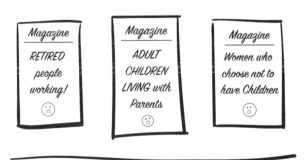

On those magazine racks, you also see reinforcements of how it's supposed to be, with a plethora of photos of celebrity weddings and births and romantic vacations. Even though significant portions of the US population do not live under this model, these are still held up as the cultural norm and the cultural narrative of how things are supposed to be and what you should be striving for. That's how you end up playing the game you've been conditioned to play.

Let's take it even further, especially the premise of the American Dream that advocates for "life, liberty, and the pursuit of happiness." If you are from the US, then you have probably been conditioned to believe that happiness comes from success, and success is defined as fame, fortune, power, and status. This leads us to pursue the *indicators* of success, which can be things like:

- Your title at work (as an indicator of fortune and power)

- How many people work for you (as an indicator of power)

- The neighborhood and home you live in (as an indicator of fortune and status)

- Where you go to school (as an indicator of future fortune and status)

- What kind of car you drive, the watch you wear, or the handbag you carry (as indicators of status and wealth)

- Where you go on vacation and how you travel there (as indicators of fame, power, status, and fortune)

- How many followers you have on social media (as an indicator of power and status)

- How many likes you get (as an indicator of power and status)

- How much access you have to others with power and influence (as an indicator of power and status)

Our common conditioning, which I think of as the love child of the Protestant work ethic and capitalism, drives us to seek those external signs of success with the hope that others will see us as successful and, as a result, their external validation will lead to our own internal validation. In other words, if others believe we're successful, hopefully we'll believe it, too, and that will make us happy!

We work hard, striving to achieve those indicators of success because we are playing the game that we have been conditioned to play.

We work hard, striving to achieve those indicators of success because we are playing the game that we have been conditioned to play. This game tells us to achieve fame and fortune and power and status and influence and a lifestyle that is considered normal just because that's what we feel we are supposed to do. It's like the fish who doesn't know it's swimming in water because that's just what it does, and it can't think of any other way it could be. Except we aren't fish. And we have choices about how to live our lives.

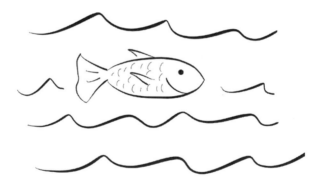

Although we normally internalize this external conditioning about what we should seek, we need to remember that it really is external. This conditioning is not necessarily who you really are, and it's not necessarily driving you to what you really want. It does not define you. Rather, it is the actual process of other people putting baggage on top of you, whether you want that baggage or not.

And it's exhausting. People make assumptions about the game you're playing based on their own conditioning and their own versions of success. This is why whenever I am invited as a successful business leader to give a talk to a group, I am inevitably asked by both men and women if I'm married and have children. I presume this is because my life and career don't fit with what others expect, so they're puzzled. I can see them trying to figure out how I could have traveled so much and lived on different continents if, as they assume, I'm married and have children.

In their efforts to figure out how my path is possible, they ask about my marital and parental status. When I respond that I am not married and don't have children, I can see them thinking, "Ohhhhh, that's why she has been able to do all of this stuff." I can see them advancing other assumptions about how I must be a workaholic or have unfulfilled longings about being married and having children.

While it's annoying to have my personal choices judged by a room full of people who are supposed to be listening to my professional insight, it's also amusing. People try to reassure me that I'm still pretty enough to get married and could still have kids, as if I must want those things and as if those things necessarily must go together. Again, this exposes people's implicit assumptions about how life is supposed to be lived and how the game is supposed to be played. And despite my preferences and the choices I've made for myself, they're trying to put me back into the traditional definition of success—into *their* mold—because that feels more comfortable for them.

Once you start paying attention, you'll notice these implicit assumptions everywhere. You'll see how many people operate under these assumptions without even realizing it, and you'll see how confused they get when you don't operate that same way. And you'll realize how many people are playing the game they've been conditioned to play.

Are You Playing Someone Else's Game?

Personally, I think all these preconceived notions about what success is supposed to be is why people have quarter-life and midlife crises. They wake up one day and say, "How the heck did I get here?!?" And they got there because they accommodated the baggage of others' expectations that was put on them and therefore they ended up playing the game they were conditioned to play, which isn't really their own game but rather someone else's that was imposed on them. Now, I must remind you that playing the game that you were conditioned to play is fine if it's what you want. Let me repeat! That game is fine if it's what *you* want for *yourself*! But it can feel suffocating if it's not the right game for you.

I'm sure you have seen this happen in people you know. In my case, my friends who are the most stressed out are those who are playing the game they've been conditioned to play rather than a game they've designed for themselves. From the outside, they show all the signs of success and winning, with lives full of beautiful weddings, huge houses, fancy private schools for their kids, expensive cars, impressive degrees from top-tier schools, important jobs, beautiful appearances, elite social statuses, and vacations in Europe.

And while some people in those situations may be fabulously happy, others are in situations where the external façade may look like the definition of "having it all." But, inside, they're unfortunately exhausted and unhappy and fighting all the time. Some people, like a few of my friends, are going through the motions, filling roles that others have conditioned them to fill, and they are resentful toward life and toward their partners and loved ones. **They're not playing the game. The game is playing them.** They're overwhelmed because they've let someone else define the rules, define the game, and define the score. And it makes me sad to be around them.

That's what it's like when you internalize this conditioning, accept the baggage that others put on you, and run yourself ragged trying to play someone else's game.

One of my students made the point that when living in another country, he felt exempt from this baggage and from others' expectations about how to live his life. And he said that perhaps this is what some people like so much about living abroad. Because you're not subjected to these expectations, you can make your own rules. You can define and play and win your own game instead of feeling forced to play someone else's game. And perhaps this is why, upon return to your home country, the reverse culture shock can be so daunting. Not only are you dealing with the changes and adjustments of reentry but you are also being subjected again to the pressures of others' expectations that you'll play their game instead of your own.

So if you decide that internalizing the conditioning and accommodating that baggage doesn't work for you, how can you remove it and start doing something that feels better to you? How do you stop playing the game that others have conditioned you to play and start playing your *own* game? And why is it so hard to change the way you think about these things? The book *Culture and Organizations* explains it this way:

> Every person carries within him- or herself patterns of thinking, feeling, and potential acting that were learned throughout the person's lifetime. Much of it was acquired in early childhood, because at that time a person is most susceptible to learning and assimilating. As soon as certain patterns of thinking, feeling, and acting have established themselves within a person's mind, he or she must unlearn these patterns before being able

to learn something different, and unlearning is more difficult than learning for the first time.[8]

Maybe we should look to the way our minds work to see why this unlearning is so difficult.

REMEMBER:

- We are all conditioned, which means you are probably playing the game someone else defined for you, and you are probably pursuing indicators of success associated with that game. But you don't have to play that game. You can choose to play a different one.

---

8   Hofstede, Hofstede, and Minkov, *Culture and Organizations*, 4–5.

CHAPTER 3

It's All in Your Head

So let's say that you're becoming aware of the idea that you've been conditioned, and you realize that maybe what you've been taught to pursue as success and what you've been pursuing aren't really working for you. You try to make changes, but it's really difficult. Let's try to understand why.

First, here's a disclaimer: I'm not a psychologist or a neuroscientist, but I've read a lot of books and articles about how our brains work, and I am going to share with you some of the things I've read that were written by other people. I'll also let you know that a friend who is a neuroscientist read this chapter, and she said that it's obviously missing nuance and scientific complexity but that it's directionally correct. If you're interested in learning more and understanding the latest scientific research, complexity, and nuances of the general thinking laid out in the pages that follow, I recommend you consult sources like *Scientific American Mind*, *Psychology Today*, *The Body Keeps the Score*, *Rewire Your Anxious Brain*, and other books and journals that are great at explaining complex scientific studies in accessible ways.

In the meantime, here's what I've learned.

Our Brains and Conditioning

Your brain is amazing, and at the most fundamental level, it is working to ensure your survival. So that's good! You should thank your brain and appreciate its efforts!

Inside your brain, you have something called the amygdala. It's generally described as the "fight or flight" part of your brain because it's associated with determining whether or not you're at risk in certain situations. When your amygdala senses danger, it sets off a series of alerts and sends signals to your adrenal glands, and adrenaline and cortisol may be released as your brain is getting your body geared up to protect you and help you get out of a situation that it is perceiving as a threat. When your amygdala is calm and doesn't perceive a threat, other cool things are going on like the release of feel-good chemicals (like oxytocin, serotonin, and dopamine), which are related to feelings of calm, happiness, and bonding.

Therefore, your brain is going to want you to do more of the things that create a state of peace and happiness, and your brain is going to want you to do less of the things that create stress and a feeling of possible danger.

Obviously your brain, and therefore the rest of you, is pretty content when things are calm, peaceful, and you're basking in a glow of happiness. And obviously your brain, and therefore the rest of you, is not very content when there is stress and possible danger lurking around.

Therefore, your brain is going to want you to do more of the things that create a state of peace and happiness, and your brain is going to want you to do less of the things that create stress and a feeling of possible danger.

How is this related to conditioning? Today, our survival is less threatened by lions and tigers and bears than it was when the amygdala was forming. But as social animals and given how our societies have developed, today, our survival is related to other humans. Think about it. We've grown food together and shared that food for survival. We've developed tribes and communities to support our social group. We have neighborhoods, schools, religious institutions, laws, family units, and other structures to ensure we cooperate, collaborate, support each other within our groups to survive and thrive. (We do not always do that across groups, but that is a different story.) Being rejected from your group can create emotional and even physical pain. Not having others to rely on for support can be very stressful for a social animal. And if you're ostracized from the group, it can feel like your very survival is at stake.

Basically the process of conditioning works within this context of our brains and through rewards and punishments from outside influences. Your brain is receiving and processing information; it's assessing whether things are OK or not. Your brain is on the lookout for threats to your survival, and this means you are constantly evaluating interactions and trying to determine if a threat, either physical or social, is present. Your brain is evaluating outside influences (including people) to determine if you should keep doing something because you get rewards and good reactions from others, which means you're safe, or if you should stop doing something because you get bad reactions and punishments from others, which means you're not safe.

Positive Feelings from Rewards

To illustrate further, I want you to think back to when you were a child and you did something great that your parent approved of. Let's say, for example, you ate your peas at mealtime and your parent praised you and let you have dessert. Between the praise and the reward of the dessert, you learned that eating peas was a good thing, and you may have even wanted to eat more peas going forward. Now, because of that praise and reward, your brain got a hit of dopamine, a feel-good chemical. You may have also gotten a warm hug from your parent over this, triggering the release of some other feel-good stuff like oxytocin, a bonding chemical, or serotonin, which is associated with lowering anxiety and boosting your mood. In any event, it felt good. And because it felt good, you and your brain wanted more, so you ate your peas and did other stuff that your parent liked for you to do because of that desire to feel good.

When you went to elementary school, those feel-good moments were related to doing well in school, with positive praise and recognition from your teacher for finishing an assignment, kudos for playing well with others at recess, and hugs from your parent for good grades and maybe even a trip to the ice cream store. Positive chemicals that made you feel good were released, and a desire to do more of those things that others wanted you to do was created because you and your brain wanted to keep getting those positive feelings.

In middle and high school, it was likely that you were still rewarded for good grades by teachers and parents, and they may have started giving you praise and rewards for your extra-curricular activities, like sports and clubs. They also may have started talking to you about grades, sports, and clubs as ways to get into a good college, setting up the expectation that they'd be so proud of you for going to college, going to a good college, and going to a good college on a scholarship.

At this point in your life, you probably also started getting positive attention from peer groups and social circles, perhaps for wearing the right kinds of clothes, making others laugh in class, giving people a ride to school, hosting parties on week-ends, dating someone great, having the most followers, or posting something that gets a lot of likes. When you did these things, your brain got hits of feel-good chemicals, and doing things that others were encouraging and wanting you to do made you feel great.

Into adulthood, the feel-good hits may have come from things like being in a romantic relationship, finding a good job, getting your own apartment, getting a promotion, getting mar-ried, having kids, buying a home, and other successes in adulting. At each phase, it was likely that your social circle—including family, friends, and colleagues—applauded you for doing these things that they wanted you to do, that they saw as normal and good and the way things are supposed to be. And this positive feedback in the form of praise and rewards from people you know and love, along with the resulting feel-good chemicals in your brain, kept you driving for more of what other people were encouraging you to go after.

Negative Feelings from Punishment

Just as you've experienced these types of rewards in your life for behaviors that are in line with what others wanted and expected from you, which made your brain very happy, you've also had punishments when you exhibited behaviors and engaged in activities that others did *not* want you to engage in. That made your brain unhappy.

When thinking about punishments, go back to when you were a child. If you did things that were dangerous, like trying to stick your finger in an electrical socket or any of the other dangerous situations that small children inadvertently put themselves in, your parent probably reacted very strongly to prevent you from doing so. You were probably stressed by their reaction and started to cry. And you may have learned to avoid sockets and other things your parents instructed you to avoid because of that negative and stressful experience.

In elementary school, you may have been reprimanded for not sharing toys, not sleeping during naptime, for disturbing other children, or for any of a variety of playground conflicts. Being reprimanded by teachers, parents, and even the principal didn't feel very good. Your brain likely perceived these as threats—to physical safety or to emotional safety—and it didn't like that feeling; therefore you sought to avoid those kinds of situations.

In fact, it felt so bad that you didn't want to repeat the behavior because you didn't want to endure the punishment again.

In middle and high school, again, the feeling of stress and punishment for undesirable behaviors may have come from parents and teachers but they also came from peers and social groups. If you were not cool (whatever that means), if you didn't hang out with the right crowd, if you got into trouble for misbehaving in the classroom or cheating on a test, if your body was going through changes that felt awkward to you and were mocked by others, or if just generally, you weren't doing what you were "supposed" to be doing, you may have received messages from people that you needed to act a different way. This most likely created stress for you. The desire to avoid the bad feelings of social rejection, of being ostracized by a friend group, of a breakup with a romantic interest, of not getting on the team, or a variety of other common situations during this phase of life may have led you to alter your behaviors to avoid those negative outcomes.

Most of us probably remember the threats of social ostracism that became prominent in middle and high school. Judgment, guilt, and shame were the tools in the arsenal of social ostracism that are used to ensure people did the expected, like wearing "appropriate" clothes, dating "appropriate" people, living in the "right" neighborhood, and driving the "right" kind of car. The judgments reflected the expectations that had become conditioned into them. And into you. Which is why you and your amygdala listened.

In the process of all of this, your brain was keeping score and wiring itself to remember which activities and behaviors were associated with positive feelings and which were associated with negative ones. When you encountered situations where you could repeat the activities and behaviors associated with positive feelings, you probably did. And when you encountered situations where you could repeat the activities and behaviors associated with negative feelings, you probably didn't. And other parts of your brain may have even gotten engaged, like the parts associated with worrying and ruminating over negative experiences. Your brain may have played out scenarios and wondered how bad something was and convinced yourself that you'd screwed up royally.

Your brain keeps score and wires itself to remember which activities and behaviors were associated with positive feelings and which were associated with negative ones.

Later on, as an adult, you may have felt stressed and feelings of punishment or failure for not getting a job that earns enough to pay for an apartment, not marrying someone, not having children, getting a divorce, not getting a promotion, not being a star on social media, not having the best abs or vacations or cars or parties, not having financial freedom, and other things that our culture's conditioning tells us are part of being a successful adult. You may have even felt judged or guilted or shamed for your choices even when doing some of these things may not have actually been associated with your version of success or with what you wanted in your life. Going to the gym everyday for great abs may not have been on your list of things that are important to you. Maybe you prefer staycations to traveling for your vacation. Maybe you didn't want to get married or you see your divorce as a blessing. Maybe you don't aspire to a promotion where you have to manage a large team and deal with the inevitable headaches associated with that. Even in those situations, your brain—because of its wiring—was probably pushing you to reconsider and to do what others seemed to expect of you.

• • •

Remember in all of this, certain behaviors and activities created positive feelings and others created negative feelings for you. Whether you felt positive or negative had to do with the reactions and expectations of *other* people. It was *others'* expectations about what was and wasn't acceptable that drove their reactions and therefore your brain's perceptions and ultimate handling of a situation.

Whether you felt positive or negative had to do with the reactions and expectations of *other* people.

If other people were pleased with what you were doing, your brain rewarded you. If other people were not, your brain punished you. Your behavior and actions were shaped accordingly, and your beliefs about what was OK and what wasn't OK were formed. That's conditioning.

And that's why it's so difficult to undo. Because through this process you were wired to pursue some things and not to pursue others. The wiring feels like instinct. It feels like it's the only way things can be. It feels like it's how it *must* be. Because of your wiring, not only do you feel like others are judging and criticizing you if you don't behave according to their expectations but you are also judging and criticizing yourself. This is why it's so difficult to pursue a different path—because your life experiences have led you to be conditioned to think there's only one right way.

But the truth is there are other ways.

And this is what fascinates me. What I learned when traveling abroad and living in some very diverse and different cultures is that not everybody is conditioned the same way. Not every culture defines behaviors and activities that need to be rewarded and behaviors and activities that need to be punished in the same way. There is not one definition of success. We have options.

Clashes in Conditioning

So much of what we're conditioned to do is so ingrained, so utterly normal and routine, that we usually don't even notice. It's only when we encounter the unexpected—a clash—that we realize there's an expectation there. We notice when someone jumps the turnstile in the subway or shows up really late to a meeting or when we run out of body wash and use shampoo instead. We notice when things don't go according to our conditioned expectations because the unexpected creates a shock, however small or large, to our system and our brains perk up and try to figure out if it's a threat or if it's something that we don't have to worry about.

It's no coincidence that most people describe their experiences of culture clashes when they are traveling abroad. This makes complete sense because these are the moments when you are interacting with people who are less likely to share your conditioning. Those from other cultures have been conditioned differently from the way you have; therefore they don't act exactly how you'd expect them to act and you're often taken aback. They may slurp their food or smoke in elevators or jump the queue. They may approach a buffet from the middle instead of from the end. They may not turn right on red—or stop at a red light at all, for that matter. They may not rush over to give you the bill at the end of your meal. They may wear clothes that you find offensive in one way or another—too modest or not modest enough. Because their conditioning is different from yours, and as a result their behaviors are different from what you expect, your brain is alerted. Your cultures seem to be clashing; but what's really clashing are the ways you've been conditioned.

Depending on the situation and on the person, people tend to react in different ways to these moments of clashes of conditioning. The reasons for different reactions aren't simply about personality and style. Rather, they have to do with how the brain is working. Some let their amygdala take over and have a bit of a freak-out while their amygdala figures out whether the situation presents a threat or not. Others are able to move into the part of the brain that controls reason and logic—the frontal lobe—and they are able to think through a situation in a calm and rational way and then make a decision about how to handle it.

When presented with a clash, you might be able to step back and say, "Hmmm, that's interesting. I wonder why that person reacted differently than what I'd expect. Isn't this a funny and amusing situation! I'm going to see what I can find out about why this is different here." If you react this way, it means the part of your brain that operates with reason and logic is probably in charge.

On the other hand, you might find yourself feeling angry in such a situation. You might say, "These stupid, rude, weird people! I'm offended and I'm going home!" In this case, it's likely that your amygdala has taken over.

Generally, it's more productive if you can recognize that a clash is happening, recognize when your amygdala is taking over, and intentionally shift your approach to put the "reason and logic" part of your brain in charge. But we're human. And it can be difficult, especially if your brain is reacting as if it's under a serious threat because someone is not acting as you'd expected them to.

The following illustration is a representation of what usually happens when people are confronted with culture clashes.[1]

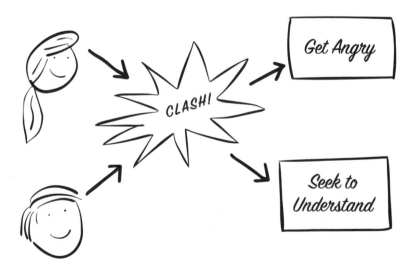

1   Graphic adapted from Duane Elmer's *Cross-Cultural Connections: Stepping Out and Fitting In around the World* (Downer's Grove, Illinois: InterVarsity Press, 2002).

Personally, I think this picture also represents any kind of situation where there's a clash of expectations, whether due to national cultures or just plain differences in conditioning where you are interacting with someone and you are not doing what the other person expects. I've been told by parents that this diagram definitely applies to life with teenagers! Whenever there are differing expectations, there are opportunities for clashes that trigger freak-outs in our brains, and opportunities for getting out of our amygdala brains where the freak-outs are occurring and into our reason and logic brains so we can move forward.

It's the same with conditioning. Much of what we do is based on that wiring; it's also based on the way our amygdala responds when we fail to do what others expect of us. When they have freak-outs, our brains may interpret this as a threat; so in an effort to be safe, often we go back to fulfilling the expectations others put on us because that feels better in the short term. It also seems easier than doing the hard work of trying to unlearn our conditioning, negotiate new expectations with ourselves and with those in our lives, and redefine our path.

So why does this matter? It helps us understand why redefining success can be so difficult. It explains for me why advice to *just stop caring about what other people think* was not helpful to me. It helps me understand there was no magic moment where everything changed for the better for me because making changes caused my brain to be uncomfortable, and therefore I'd often slide back to previous types of behaviors because they felt more comfortable.

As Hofstede et al. said, "Unlearning is more difficult than

learning."[2] But some of the latest work in neuroplasticity suggests that our brains can learn new ways if they are exposed to new types of experiences.[3] Although our brains may prefer *not* to be rewired, learning and change occur when we open ourselves up to letting that happen. Instead of getting stuck in your ruts and routines, you can bring in new experiences, get above your amygdala, move your thinking into your frontal lobe, and use logic, reason, and choice to begin to define success differently. It's not easy, but it can be done. In the next chapter, I'll share with you my own experience in doing it.

REMEMBER:

- Your brain wants to protect you and keep you safe, and it has been wired to assess all sorts of threats. Redefining and pursuing your own version of success may feel threatening and require you to deal with your own brain's freak-outs—as well as those of others.

---

2 Geert Hofstede, Gert Jan Hofstede, and Michael Minkov, *Culture and Organizations: Software of the Mind* (New York: McGraw-Hill Education, 2010), 5.

3 Genevieve Fox, "Meet the neuroscientist shattering the myth of the gendered brain," *The Guardian*, Feb 24, 2019.

CHAPTER 4

Spending the Most Amount of Time in the Coolest Places

T his is my own personal game: I don't really care what I do professionally as long as I get to do it while interacting with people from different cultures. I have hawked tampons and toilet paper and cell phones and data services, and in doing so, I have traveled to more than 60 countries, lived and worked on 4 continents, and flown almost 4 million miles in my life.

Now, I didn't always know that I wanted this life of travel to be my game, but I have always had an interest in different cultures and different ways of life. I grew up in a very small town in Florida that did not have much diversity except in the variety of swamp critters we had in our backyard. Through student council at my school, I had opportunities to travel to different parts of the state for workshops and conferences. We would get in a van with our teachers and drive for 8, 10, or 12 hours to get to the meetings. I loved those trips and was so struck by how different the kids from South Florida were from people from my part of the state, and I was drawn to the Miami crowd in particular because they spoke Spanish. It was like they had access to a whole world that no one else understood. Literally. I was fascinated by them!

Fortunately through student council, I got to go to New Mexico with one of my teachers for a big conference and I met the West Coasters with their surfer clothes and skateboards and the Texans with their cowboy boots and hats who seemed like they came straight out of the movies. And during my junior year of high school, there was an opportunity to go to Russia for three weeks in December. I needed to earn money to pay for the trip, so I got a job at an ice cream parlor and worked all summer. The trip was incredible, but I froze my ass off because the Florida version of cold-weather clothes didn't cut it in Russia! But I loved every minute of it. We got to meet with college students, visit historical sites, and hear about history and politics from their perspective, which didn't always align to the versions I was being taught in my US school.

During high school and college, I realized through these and other trips to places like Germany and Italy and Mexico that we're all on this planet trying to do more or less the same thing—eat, work, have some dignity, and have good relationships with other people—but we organize ourselves to do that in very different ways. This realization led me to study religion, politics, economics, anthropology, sociology, languages, and art history. And as I got older, I found that the world of business offered opportunities for me to explore those fascinating aspects of our world—not just in an intellectual way but as a participant as well.

Playing the Game I Was Taught to Play

While I was traveling and learning and exploring in my teens and twenties, I was also definitely playing the game that others expected me to play. I studied hard, pursued higher education at great universities, got married, got a job at a corporation, and started climbing the corporate ladder. I traveled in business class or on private planes, I stayed at amazing hotels and ate at the best restaurants in the world, I interacted with C-level executives at Fortune 100 companies, and I helped drive growth and change at work.

On the outside, I was ticking off all the boxes that others had taught me I needed to be ticking off. The external rewards and recognition felt great, and there were a lot of dopamine hits with all of that excitement and applause. Internally, however, it was a bit of a different story. The focus on work and the traveling definitely contributed to stresses at home, but more fundamentally, after eight years of marriage, my husband and I were starting to diverge in terms of what we were seeing for our life together.

This divergence came to a head when I received an offer to move to Argentina for a great new job. He wanted to be supportive so we sold our home, put our dog on an airplane and our furniture on a boat, and moved far, far away. His employer had made accommodations for him to work from abroad, and it seemed like we had all the puzzle pieces in place.

But it was hard. Argentina was in a moment of economic, political, and social crisis, which certainly didn't help. After a few months, my husband decided that he didn't want to stay in Argentina and he returned to the US. He encouraged me to stay and finish out my assignment, after which his plan was for me to move back to the US where we would buy a house and start a family.

My spouse started expressing more interest in having children, and while I liked the idea in the abstract, I feared the reality. Some of this was for medical reasons. I'd been told I would need to start fertility treatments to be able to get pregnant and that I'd likely have a difficult pregnancy due to some other medical issues. Even more than that, I didn't think that having children would allow me to be the kind of parent I would have wanted to be while also pursuing my passions of traveling and working abroad. Quite frankly, I didn't want to give up the travel, and I didn't want to screw up my kids. My own implicit assumption in my twenties was that traveling would somehow screw up my unborn children, which I now know was just my conditioning in action.

It was also clear that my spouse was up for adventure, but of a different variety. I wanted the international kind, and he wanted the domestic version. Because of these differences, one of the hardest choices of my life was thrust upon me and I separated from my spouse. I did not do this well. I could not articulate what was happening. I created pain for others and endured pain myself. It was chaotic and sad and depressing; and my amygdala was definitely telling me to play it safe and stay married. At the time I could not express it, but looking back now, somehow my frontal lobe knew that a relationship where two people had a desire to go on very different paths could not thrive. Both would feel suffocated and resentment could build, which would erode whatever positive feelings the relationship had been built on in the first place. It's easier to say that now, but at the time it felt like an earthquake and a volcano and a tsunami and a tornado all wrapped into one.

Making choices about divorce is difficult, and it goes back to the conditioning and the way your brain reacts, which I talked about in the previous chapters. The overall conditioned expectation that we share is that a normal life includes getting married, having kids, living in a house with those kids together, staying married, and growing old with your spouse. That's the "happily ever after" at the end of all the fairy tales and rom-com movies that we've all seen, heard, read, and internalized.

When you talk about getting married and having kids, everybody is super happy and supportive and cheers you on because you're doing what they expect you to do. There are lots of dopamine hits. Then when you talk about getting divorced, it makes people very uncomfortable because you are doing something unexpected. They start talking to you about how bad divorce is, they start judging you for it, and your amygdala gets triggered.

I Needed Therapy

After my divorce, I was still living in Argentina, where I spent two years in a state of depression and shock and paralysis wondering, "What have I done?" I was going through the motions and going to work every day, but my mental state was fragile because basically I had pulled the rug out from under myself. I did not know if I was going to be OK, I did not really have anyone to rely on, my amygdala was in a constant state of agitation, and my body was in a state of stress. I got sick a lot, I lost too much weight, I was always tired, and quite frankly, I was unwell. I needed therapy.

I needed therapy to be able to give myself permission to go after what I really wanted professionally and personally without defining that through the lens of what others had expected from me, of what others told me I was supposed to want, or of what others wanted me to do for them.

And I went through therapy not because it was fun—it wasn't—but because it started feeling like my literal survival depended on bucking the trends that I had been conditioned to embrace. Unraveling the conditioning, figuring out what I wanted without the baggage of what others wanted for me, and finding the strength to pursue my own path and design my own game without concern for others' judgment took a while. And trust me . . . there is judgment. Even just the decision to go to therapy can often be met with judgment because there's a stigma attached. If you're going to therapy, people think that means something must be wrong with you.

Fortunately during the years in Argentina, I learned to embrace therapy. Argentines love it. Everyone has a therapist. Everyone talks about going to therapy. Someone once told me there were more therapists per capita in Argentina than any-where else in the world; and although I don't have the data to prove that, I believe it! Argentines go to therapy even when things are going well, so I decided to go too. I also went while I was living in Hong Kong where it's not so common. And I still go now that I am based again in the US. Personally, I think everybody should go and they should go regularly, not just when they're in crisis. I consider it "monthly mental maintenance," just like the maintenance of getting my hair cut or my nails done.

During therapy, I realized that the professional life I wanted to lead had to do with living, working, and traveling to different countries and interacting with other cultures, and I realized I wanted to do that in a corporate business environment. Person-ally, I realized that I wanted to prioritize healthy friendships and romantic relationships with people who were not critical or judgmental of me and my choices.

This may sound simple now, but it took a lot of time to get there because I'd been taught to prioritize having a husband and letting him take the lead, minimizing myself and my career for his, and dedicating my life to raising kids. The process of rewrit-ing this definition of success and overall life narrative was big.

Getting the Right Kind of Support

Once I figured that out, I chose to cultivate friendships with people who had also redefined success and rewritten their own narratives. I sought out people who were playing their own games instead of people who were playing the game we had all been conditioned to play. And I asked for their support to help me follow my own new path.

In the process, I had to let go of some friends whose support took the form of trying to mold me to follow their conditioned paths. For example, some friends kept trying to set me up with someone so I could get married again. Others tried to convince me that my internal searching would be solved by having a baby. And I didn't speak to one particular close friend for a year after she told me, "I just don't know why no one wants to marry you, because you're so great." I wasn't mad at her but that comment definitely hit me hard and caused a freak-out in my brain, and it took a long time for me to unpack why that comment was so difficult for me to hear. Was it because I felt unworthy? Or because it sounded like I was a product on the shelf that was there for someone to buy? Or that my worth came from someone else choosing me?

All of these were doozies, which is why it took me so long to realize that my friend likes to be married; so if she were in a situation where she wasn't married, that would make *her* feel bad. Because she doesn't want *me* to feel bad, she was projecting her view of where happiness comes from onto me. Once I figured that out, I called her and we talked about it and hugged over the phone—and to be honest, I think both of us feel closer now, like we know each other better and can support each other better because of it.

And I don't want to minimize this, because letting go of people is really difficult. Some people who love you very much may encourage you to follow a certain path and to play the game that you've been conditioned to play because they think it will be "easier" for you. And it may seem easier. Until you realize that it's harder to be someone you're not than it is to be the person you want to be. Being honest with them and trying to get the support you need from them is important to be able to move forward.

Some people who love you very much may encourage you to follow a certain path and to play the game that you've been conditioned to play because they think it will be "easier" for you.

It also means supporting others on their journeys in the ways they need to be supported. For one of my friends, it meant supporting him as he went against the grain and quit the "big" job to start a home renovation business. For another work friend, it meant supporting him as he was coming out and other colleagues were uncomfortable with it. When I was at dinner one evening with these colleagues, who were from Mexico, Peru, and Puerto Rico, they were saying that they thought he should have stayed in the closet because it would have been easier for him than coming out. I remarked that perhaps it was easier for him to come out than to keep hiding and pretending to be someone he was not—or as Anaïs Nin wrote more eloquently, "And the day came when the risk to remain tight in a bud was more painful than the risk it took to blossom." And they looked at me like I had three heads. Then one said, "I've never thought of it that way before." And everyone went back to eating their food.

These men had been conditioned that anything other than heterosexuality was a deviation from the norm, and that it was a choice. Therefore they couldn't understand why anyone would choose to be anything other than heterosexual, because it was inviting judgment into their lives. So they were puzzled when our colleague came out and thought that it would have been easier for him to stay in the closet. They'd never even considered that living a lie would be more difficult for that colleague, and they'd never even considered that they could have chosen to define "normal" as "doing what is right for you and in keeping with who you are." But instead, they followed their conditioning and defined "normal" as "doing what others expect." Their understanding of the world plus some good old-fashioned homophobia led them to be very uncomfortable and also judgmental of our colleague.

Instead of arguing with them and telling them they were ridiculous, which is what I wanted to do, I moved into my frontal lobe and presented them with an alternative—that living a lie was more difficult than coming out. And they paused, and I swear I could see their frontal lobes click on in the way they looked at me and considered what I said. I don't think I changed anyone's mind, and just because you present an alternate perspective to someone doesn't mean they're going to accept it and change quickly. But I like to present it anyway because at least it makes them stop and think that there's more than just one way.

Finding a New Way

After getting some clarity in therapy about what I wanted professionally and personally and surrounding myself with supportive people, I got to work to make big changes in my life. During this time, I worked on language skills, flexibility, and cultural competence. And I decided to only accept jobs that have a component of international work and that include travel. I spent significant amounts of time in Asia, Europe, Latin America, and the Middle East, and I strove to have regular experiences rather than touristic ones. I sought to understand how the cultures work, including observing and understanding key aspects of conditioning and of social structures, norms, and narratives in various places around the world.

In doing so, I learned about other cultures, but I also developed the ability to reflect more on my own culture and conditioning. I started writing and created a blog. Eventually I created a course about how to lead and communicate more effectively in different cultures, which I got to teach at a leading business school.

I'm Playing My Own Game Now

With clarity about my objectives and the obstacles to getting there, and thanks to Gail Evans's book explaining that this is all just a game anyway, I've been playing my own game ever since, with my own rules and my own scoreboard, which tracks the cool places I get to spend time in each year.

I've changed companies and industries several times, and I have moved continents on various occasions. But I have always ensured that I was working internationally and traveling to cool places. As my home base, I have chosen a city in the US with an awesome airport and direct flights to pretty much anywhere in the world. My sister and parents are nearby so they can keep an eye on each other when I'm traveling, and I can enjoy time with them when I'm home. That's not an accident. It's by design.

When I speak at universities and professional associations, I get a lot of questions about my personal life. It's as if people see me, listen, and then feel the need to make my life choices fit their implicit assumptions, conditioning, and beliefs. This often doesn't work, because I don't fit most people's preconceived notions about what successful people look like or how they live. They keep asking questions until their frontal lobes engage and they can reconcile what they see with what I've been saying. In case you have been having trouble reconciling it too, here are the questions I get asked most frequently with my very honest responses:

- **Do I have to work?** Of course I do. And not just to pay the bills but to keep my busy self challenged and entertained. And I choose the type of work I do based on how well it will help me accomplish the objective of my game, which is to interact and understand different cultures and countries.

- **Is it all glitz and glam?** Of course it's not. Airport delays, complexities of multicultural work, and time zones can all drain my energy at times. Then there's the regular stuff at work related to deadlines and pressure to deliver on results and fix problems. And at home, there are issues like being out of town for a friend's birthday party or trying to deal with a repairman's schedule that doesn't coincide with mine and the regular packing, unpacking, and repacking of my suitcase. But my life is mine. It's how I've designed it and it's how I want it to be.

- **Will the way I play my game evolve?** Hell, yes! I hope to start spending one or two months at a time in my favorite places around the world and to strategically time those stays to avoid cold winters. I also envision a future with more nonprofit work with an international organization as well as speaking and advising engagements at universities and professional associations.

- **Have I been passed over for promotions?** Absolutely. Do I care? I won't lie. That part can be frustrating—until I remember that I'm playing my own game and that some of those promotions would have taken away my ability to do so.

- **Have my relationships been impacted?** Yup. Not everybody is looking for a partner who travels frequently. And I understand that. Some people thrive on the day-to-day interaction and rhythm, which gets interrupted when one person is gone a lot. But others seem to like time together and time to miss each other. The relationships I have had have been great because I am me, playing my own game instead of warping myself into the person someone else wants me to be. And I'd like to think that the people with whom I've been involved have appreciated the honesty and authenticity of the relationship. (Except for one. Ouch.)

- **Do I have kids?** Nope. I don't even have a pet or plants. But I enjoy the hell out of other people's kids and pets and plants. And I enjoy time away from their kids and pets and plants too.

- **Do I regret not having children?** No. Full stop. And just writing that makes some of you uncomfortable because people are "supposed" to want to have children; and if they don't, there must be something wrong with them. That is conditioning at its finest. Some people are dying to have children, some aren't so excited about the idea, and others really don't want to. And I think all of those options are OK.

- **Is it easier to make these choices because I don't have children?** Absolutely. And that's by design. That's my choice because I'm playing my own game.

- **Am I worried about who will take care of me when I'm old?** Those of you asking this question are assuming that everybody lives a long time, that children always take care of their elderly parents, that children are the best caregivers, and that parents always need taking care of. Look at how many assumptions are in there about how things are supposed to be! And the answer is no. I'm not worried.

- **Am I going to have a work-free retirement?** I hope not! I hope my life will just keep morphing into new, different, interesting experiences.

- **Does it ever get tiring?** Sometimes. Even professional athletes have an off-season to rest. Sometimes I need to take a break from travel and sit somewhere for a month or so. Then I'm raring to go again. Because it's who I am. It's what I want. It's what I've designed for myself. It's my own game. And it makes me happy.

- **Has anyone told me no?** Not yet. And if they do, I'll just make some different choices. I will keep playing my game instead of being restricted by the games that others want me to play. Does that mean I'll walk into work one day and say, "Screw you," and walk out? Nope. But it does mean that whenever I've seen options become limited due to corporate restructuring or changes in strategic directions, I start mapping out my new plans. It may take 3, 6, or 12 months to make these new plans happen, but they always happen. I always get back to my game.

- **Will I play a different game someday?** Maybe. And if I do, it will be because I choose to. And whatever it is, it will be great because I will design it that way.

- So now that you know the game that I am playing, let's get focused on how you can play your own game too.

REMEMBER:

- Redefining success for you, finding the right kinds of support, and playing your own game feels really good.

CHAPTER 5

What Game Are You Playing Today?

A lthough conceptually it may sound simple, sometimes it can be really difficult to get your head around thinking of your life as a game and understanding how to make it work for you. After all, we're talking about your personal, professional, and life choices—and all the hopes, dreams, realities, and responsibilities to yourself and others that have gone into making those choices. How do you link those things together so that they reinforce each other to help you pursue your own game and live the life you want?

In this book, we'll use a simple four-part framework as the organizing principle for your game. You'll become familiar with the four parts of the framework and understand how they fit together over the next few chapters. The four parts are:

- Your game's objective, which refers to what you're pursuing;
- How you play your game, and what kinds of moves you make;
- What obstacles must be overcome, including both internal and external challenges; and
- How to keep score so you know that you're winning.

It looks like this.

WHAT IS THE OBJECTIVE?

HOW DO YOU PLAY?

WHAT ARE THE OBSTACLES?

HOW DO YOU KEEP SCORE?

It's important for us to begin with your current state, so in the next pages, you'll have the opportunity to reflect on some key questions that will help you fill out this framework based on how you're living your life and defining your success today. I don't want you to get too hung up on the framework yet. Just let your thoughts flow based on the questions asked in this chapter without worrying too much about organizing them. After you've reflected on your current state, we'll use the framework to define your future state and the new game that you can play to redefine success for you. Then you can focus on playing the hell out of that game so you can achieve what matters most to you.

In the next chapter, where you will define your new game, we'll start with your objective. But what I've found is that it's often difficult for people to articulate the objective of their current game right off the bat. I think that's because most of us are pursuing what we've been trained or taught to do, so it doesn't even feel like a conscious choice—it just feels like what we're supposed to be doing and we assume everyone else is doing it as well.

So to get you warmed up and going, we are going to start with the second part of the framework: How are you playing your game? This is so you can ponder on what you are doing in your life. How are you spending your time? How are you playing your game?

How Are You Playing Your Game Today?

Start by thinking about your daily life. Just a regular, usual day. What does it look like for you? Do you get up at 7 a.m., leave the house at 8 a.m. to drive to work by 9 a.m., work on a computer in an office, eat lunch at your desk or in the company cafeteria, leave by 5 p.m. to avoid traffic, get home, make dinner for the kids, and crash in front of the TV by 9 p.m.? Or do you wake up at 10 a.m., shower, eat, and get to your first class at noon, go play basketball at 6 p.m., study until midnight, then dive into a video game until 2 a.m.? Or maybe you wake up at 5 a.m. to have some time to yourself before your kids wake up and the morning rush to get them to school starts. Or maybe you work in the mornings and go to school at night.

Whatever it is, write it down. What does your daily life look like?

YOUR DAILY LIFE

6 AM ———————————————

————————————————————————

————————————————————————

————————————————————————

————————————————————————

————————————————————————

———————————————————

————————————————————

————————————————————————

————————————————————————

————————————————————————

2 AM ———————————————

Head to Gutsy.world/resources to download these charts in a larger, printable format.

Most of us talk about our lives and our games by saying how busy we are. We often talk about what we're doing every day and how exhausted we are by it. The choices you're making every day are choices about how to play your game. They may or may not be connected to your big objective, however; and this framework will help make disconnects visible to you.

Now that you're warmed up and you've defined what you are doing, which is how you play your game, let's focus on *why* you are doing those things. This is related to the objective part of the framework. What objective are you pursuing in your current game? Let's dive in.

What's Your Objective?

Think about whom you're trying to please in your life. Who are you trying to make happy and how? This one may be a little more difficult because you may have many people on your list. Maybe you are trying to make your boss happy with great work, your significant other happy by being present and attentive or getting the oil changed in the car, and your kids or your parents happy as well. Maybe you're focused on pleasing your friends and getting likes on social media and making them laugh in school. Or maybe it's your neighbors with your beautiful lawn. Or maybe you're even trying to please people you don't even really know because you are worrying about what other people will think. Maybe you're trying to make yourself happy, like my friend who I visited recently who told me, "I can't pick you up at the airport because your flight lands when I'm having a mani-pedi." And I thought, *Good for her! She's making sure to please herself along with others!*

Reflect for a few moments on whom you're trying to please and how you're trying to do so. Write it down.

WHO ARE YOU TRYING TO PLEASE? AND HOW?

Now I want you to look back at your worksheet and consider the question of *whom* you are trying to please as well as *what* you are pursuing in order to please them. Ask yourself if what you are pursuing in order to please those people is based on what they've told you or based on what you've assumed about what they want from you. It's a deep and fundamental question because sometimes we are working our butts off to please others, only to find out that we're doing something that's not really all that important to them.

In my marriage, my partner and I both were exhausted trying to do things for each other, but neither of us felt like the other person was giving us what we needed because, fundamentally, neither of us understood what was important to the other person. So ask yourself if what you're doing is because of something that you're sure about due to good communication between you and others in your life or if you're doing it because you're assuming it is important to them and you are therefore pursuing it with vigor without checking with them to be sure it's what they want.

When you think about what you're doing to please yourself, consider what the deeper needs are that you're trying to satisfy. For example, my friend mentioned previously who prioritizes her manicures and pedicures doesn't really care that much about her fingernails and toenails. She's really trying to engage in some self-care, because between work and her kids and family obligations with her mom and nephew, she gets very little time to herself. So she's trying to please herself with mani-pedis while she is also pleasing a lot of other people by caring for them and their needs. Alternatively, perhaps you're driving toward financial goals to please yourself because you have a deeper need to feel secure and you focus on saving money and paying off debt as a result. Whatever it may be, think about what you're doing to make yourself happy and ponder the deeper need that is driving your behavior.

Take some extra time to reflect and be really honest with yourself about what you are pursuing as well as what your underlying motivations may be. You may find that you are driven by someone else's voice in your head—a parent or a significant other or a former teacher or a current boss, for example. You may find that you are doing a lot to please other people without realizing it. And you may discover that you are not doing enough to take care of and please yourself.

When you're ready, let's move on to the next part of the framework, which deals with the obstacles that will arise as we pursue our objectives.

What Are the Obstacles?

The third question to reflect on is related to the obstacles and frustrations you are facing in your life today. What are the things that create stress and deplete your energy on a daily basis? Whether it's lack of time, lack of sleep, lack of resources, lack of help, lack of knowledge about a particular topic, that stupid boss or coworker, your demanding family member, your ungrateful friend, horrible traffic, your car that needs repairs, or your upstairs neighbor, write it down. What are the things you are having to deal with to get through your day? Go ahead. Take some time to vent and rant. Get it all out.

WHAT *OBSTACLES* ARE YOU FACING?

On a daily basis, I hear from friends, colleagues, and students about how stressed they are in their lives. The factors that cause stress are obstacles. For instance, one friend has shared an ongoing saga at her work where her boss's boss has been asking her for feedback about her boss. Apparently others have complained to Human Resources about her direct boss, and given the trust that more senior leaders have in my friend, they are asking her for the lowdown. Obviously this puts my friend in a terribly awkward situation of giving negative feedback about her boss to superiors and dealing with potential retaliation as her boss becomes aware. This is an obstacle of working in a toxic workplace, and she is absorbing undue stress as a result.

Here's another example: Several colleagues who are early in their careers have complained to me about lack of sleep. They're seriously exhausted because they are balancing work, school, and social lives. And they refuse to give up on their social lives, which I applaud. They have so many projects and initiatives and deadlines, and they're frightened of falling behind on any of them because they're worried that others will get ahead of them or that they'll be left behind and be considered and feel like failures. Their obstacles are related to embracing a timeline that imposes deadlines on their lives, like finishing college by 22, having two years of work experience and an MBA by 26, getting married by 29, buying a home at 30, having a first child by 32 and a second by 34, paying off student loans by 35, and retiring early at 45. The timelines are often self-imposed and derived from comparing themselves to others; and this is at the heart of the obstacle about lack of sleep—trying to do too much really fast to "beat" someone else by arriving at a life milestone faster than they do.

Others share with me their frustrations with traffic and wasting two hours per day sitting in a parking lot of an interstate with thousands of fellow city dwellers. The obstacle here is that they have to actually show their faces in their offices at the same time every day, even though many of them could be working remotely or showing up an hour later with little detriment to their performance.

So when you're looking at obstacles and frustrations, take time to vent about the more superficial things (like why my dishwasher has been broken for two months and still isn't fixed). But then look deeper about what those things represent to figure out what the real obstacles are (like I travel a lot, so coordinating with a repairman seems impossible).

I suggest you pause for a few minutes and gather your thoughts. Sometimes we can get overwhelmed by the quantity of obstacles so try to think about which ones are just annoyances and which ones really get in your way. Then when you're ready, we'll move on to the last part, which deals with keeping score.

How Do You Keep Score?

Finally, start thinking about how you measure your own success. How are you currently keeping score? What are the tangible and intangible things in your life that you keep track of to determine whether or not you are successful? Write them down.

How do you keep SCORE?

If it's difficult to figure out, maybe start with the tangible things, like your bank account, your handbag or watch collection, where you vacation, or how many frequent flyer miles you have. Maybe consider whether you measure success by how many followers and connections and friends you have on social media, or perhaps by the number of concerts you've seen live, or the beauty of your garden compared to your neighbor's, or your marathon personal record, or how many times a week you go to the gym. What are the things you strive for, check in on, and try to get more of?

I have friends who day trade, and every single day they measure their success by how their investments have been doing. In truth, they're not only measuring their financial situation but also their wit, their smarts, their ability to read the market, make decisions, take risks, and reap rewards from their activities.

Others measure their success physically—by how much weight they can lift, how fast they can run, how defined their muscles are, or how many of the latest and greatest new fitness trends they've tried compared to other people. Some of my friends compete pretty intensely about how many countries and cities they've visited and how exotic their vacations are. And parents sometimes measure their success through their kids' achievements. These are the parents showing up to all of their kids' sporting events and yelling at the coaches and referees and opposing team players. They're the ones pushing their kids to achieve more in music and academics and driving their kids toward getting accepted at great colleges because they perceive that to be a measure of successful parenting.

You may also be measuring your success in intangible ways,

like how much free time you have, if you get to skip out of work

How do you measure success? Be honest with yourself. early or avoid the office and work from home. You may note the peace and calm you feel on weekends or the joy you feel when your kids or nieces or nephews visit.

How you measure success is up to you. Be honest with yourself. No one really knows your answers except for you. Go back to your page, and write down the big ways you keep score.

Evaluating Your Current Game

Now let's put it all together and reflect on your current game to see how well the pieces fit. How well is your objective aligned to how you are playing your game? Are you aware of the obstacles and working to overcome them? Are you keeping score on the stuff that matters most to you?

As you reflect on those questions and your answers, what are the things in your life that make you smile and feel joy deep in your heart? Are they academic or professional achievements and recognition? Are they the new luxury items you purchased, which are evidence of a job well done to you and to others? Are they the positive feelings you get when you've learned something new and grown personally or professionally? Are they the moments of free time where you get to sing and dance and laugh? Are they moments when you've helped someone in need? Are they moments with loved ones during the holidays or on vacations? What are the things that bring you joy and stand out as memorable to you? Recognizing these things will help you define your future game.

What are the parts that feel like burdens? When you were going through these exercises, were the financial stresses of a big house or fancy car or student debt feeling like burdens you'd like to rid yourself of? Were there people at your workplace—coworkers or bosses or others—who brought up negative and toxic feelings for you? Were there feelings that certain family members or friends were judging or criticizing you or putting expectations on you that you did not want? Or perhaps it's something else for you? Hang on to those feelings, as they're also important for designing your new game.

As you continue to reflect on your worksheets and on those questions mentioned previously, you will start to realize that these are the core questions that will help you create a new game moving forward.

As a reminder, the following figure is what it looks like when we put it together.

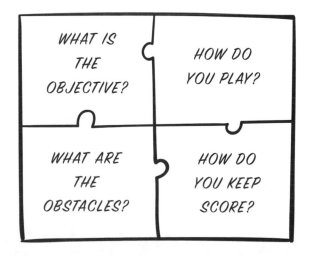

Think about the worksheets you just completed, and use them to analyze the game you're currently playing. For example, look again at your answers for the worksheet where you listed the people you are trying to please and how. Is an overarching objective emerging from what you've written? Is there a clear focus on what you are pursuing in your life today? It's OK if you don't have one. Most people don't, because they're just going through the motions and doing what others expect of them without really giving it much thought. I hope you'll continue to use this worksheet, reflect further, and differentiate between what you are doing to make others happy and what you are doing that actually makes *you* happy.

In the worksheet where you wrote down what your daily life looks like, take a look at what you wrote and ask yourself if there is a link between how you're spending your time and what you've said you were trying to do to please yourself and others. Is there consistency between what you're doing all day and who you are trying to please and how?

Now, with all of this in mind, take a look at the list of obstacles that you wrote down. What are the big things getting in the way of your ability to achieve objectives of pleasing yourself and others that you wrote down? What is getting in your way of doing more of what makes you and those you care about happy? Are you consciously doing anything to overcome those obstacles?

And lastly, look at where you listed your measures of success. Are the things you are measuring really related to your ultimate objective of making yourself and those you care about happy?

Are there better ways to measure your success based on what is really important for you?

Some really great friends and family members have shared with me their worksheets about the game they're playing today. And they allowed me to share them with you. Take a look.

This friend works in finance in a corporate environment, which is the epitome of the rat race.

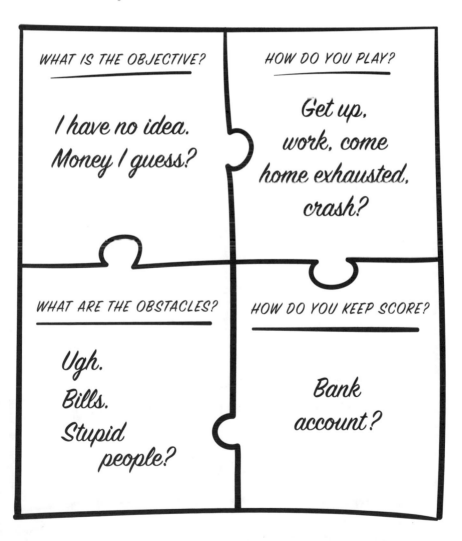

And this friend works in marketing and has two small children.

WHAT IS THE OBJECTIVE?

Hold it all together—kids, marriage, work.

HOW DO YOU PLAY?

One, hectic, exhausting day at a time.

WHAT ARE THE OBSTACLES?

Exhaustion
Poopy diapers
My boss. Ugh.

HOW DO YOU KEEP SCORE?

Still married.
Kids alive.
Clothes still fit.

What does your game look like today? Draw it here.

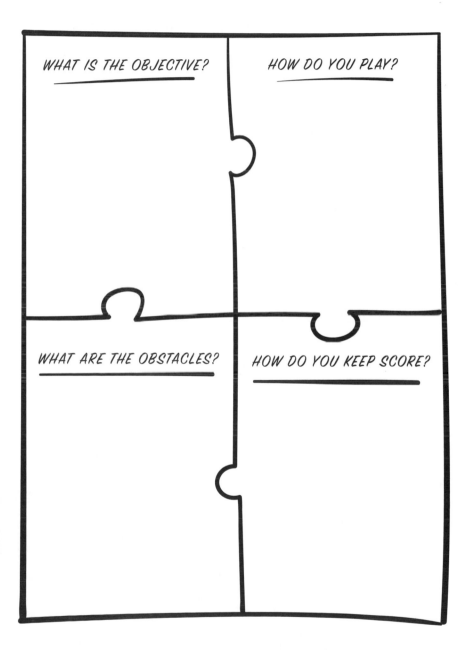

If your current game looks like most people's, there may be objectives that are statistically unlikely or unattainable. For instance, for my colleague who burst into my office and inspired this whole book, the game of "Making the Most Money in the Company" is a game that only one person can win, so statistically that's a game that's pretty tough. If your goal is to have the nicest house in the neighborhood, statistically that's also pretty tough to win. So instead of playing games like those that you're probably going to lose, why not create your own game instead? If you're going to expend the energy, why play a game that's going to kick your ass when you can play a game you're going to rock?

Why play a game that's going to kick your ass when you can play a game you're going to rock?

Now that you recognize the game you've already been playing, you can also become more aware of which parts you want to change or eliminate and which parts you want to keep for your future game. That's what we'll get focused on in the next chapter.

REMEMBER:

- Gaining awareness of what you are doing and why will help you redefine success, design your future game, and rock at it!

CHAPTER 6

Designing a New Game

N ow that you've outlined your current game and reflected on whether or not you'd like to make some changes, you're ready to design your new game. Let's look more closely at the four major aspects of the framework you need to consider. These are complementary to the worksheets you did in chapter 5, but now we are going to define each part of your game intentionally and look toward the future. Here you will design a new game that redefines success around what you actually want in life, rather than looking at how you're playing your current game. Here's a reminder of the framework we will use:

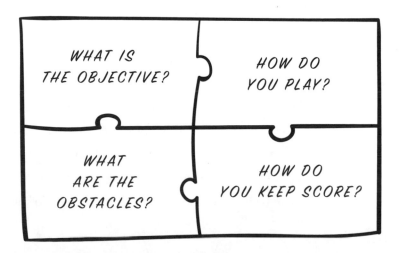

And remember, here's what each step focuses on:

1. **What is your objective?** What do you want? What do *you* want? This is often the most difficult because it requires soul-searching, honesty, and courage.

2. **How do you play your game?** Basically, how do you spend your time, talents, and resources to achieve your objectives?

3. **What obstacles must be overcome?** What are the blockers that are keeping you from playing your game? Usually these are things like fear, the need for new skills, people who are trying to hold you back, or the need for supporters.

4. **How do you keep score to know that you're winning?** How will you keep track to ensure that you're actually playing your game and winning? What will your points be? And what will your scoreboard look like?

Let's dive into that first question, as it's the deepest and usually the most difficult.

What Will Your Objective Be?

What do *you* want? Not what you think you're supposed to want, not what others want for you, not what others want for themselves, but what do *you* want?

In order to figure this out, it takes reflection and some understanding about where your own real happiness comes from. This part is difficult because it requires shedding a lifetime of layers of others' expectations and figuring out what's important to you.

Because this can be hard to grasp at first, a good place to start is to think about what others want *for* you and what they want *from* you rather than thinking about what you want for yourself. After all, most of us have been conditioned that thinking about what we want for ourselves is selfish and, therefore, bad. Asking the question from a different angle and taking a different approach can lead to a fresh perspective on why we do the things we do. Do we do them because it's what we really want, or is it that we're trying to please someone else, or maybe we are trying to want what we're supposed to want?

Take some time to ponder this, and start by asking yourself:

- What did you learn from your parents? What did they want for you? What did they want from you?
- What about your romantic interests?
- Your friends?
- Your teachers?
- Religious leaders in your life?
- Your boss?
- Colleagues?
- That amorphous group of "they" that is comprised of societal expectations that you learned from movies, TV, magazines, websites, and the news?

Write it all down here.

WHO	WHAT THEY WANT FOR YOU	WHAT THEY WANT FROM YOU	WHY

Spend some time on this and reflect. Then come back tomorrow and revise it, because it's important to have clarity about what it is *you* really want and expect out of life and what expectations are put on you by *others*.

As you examine what you've written down, ask yourself how much of what all these people wanted for you was based on what made *them* happy and therefore they assume that's what will make *you* happy too. Maybe someone in your family is very happy as a lawyer, and therefore they want you to be a lawyer too. Maybe someone has built a family business and they want to pass it down to you because they want you to feel the pride that they feel of owning a business. Maybe someone has been happy living in a city by the mountains and they want you to share their love of camping and hiking. Sometimes people want for you what they've found to be good for them.

> It's important to have clarity about what *you* want and expect out of life and what expectations are put on you by *others*.

Then ask yourself how much of what they want for you is based on what made them unhappy and therefore something they want you to avoid. Maybe someone hated working in a corporate environment and always wanted to be an entrepreneur, so they encourage you to start a company. Maybe someone owned a restaurant that struggled or failed so they discourage your culinary interests. Or maybe someone had a terrible romantic relationship and they advise you not to trust anyone.

In these cases, recognize that people in your life are trying to encourage you and give you advice on things that have and haven't worked for them out of a desire to help you and make your life easier. But their advice may not work for you, so it's good to reflect and understand where their perspectives are coming from and then decide if it's helpful for you or not.

And ask yourself how much is based on what you can do to make *their* lives easier, which is what they want *from* you, not *for* you. This is important because sometimes people in our lives are not looking out for our best interests and they are more concerned about looking out for their own interests through us. These are people who want you to take on their burdens—whether it's financial support from you while they're not working (and they never plan to work), expectations that you'll perform domestic duties at a greater rate than they do, or just general expectations that you'll manage family life and other matters for them. These are people who are more interested in how you're serving them than in how you're mutually supporting each other. And these are people who you may want to consider distancing yourself from.

Normally people want for you what has worked for them. And they want you to avoid the things that didn't work for them. That's because they want what they think is best for you. But when listening to their advice, remember that *you* decide what is best for you. They don't. Keep looking at what you've written in your worksheet, and then take some time to reflect again—not just on the people in your worksheet but on the content of what they want *for* you and what they want *from* you.

Normally people want for you what has worked for them. And they want you to avoid the things that didn't work for them.

As you were writing, did you notice what felt great and what felt like a burden? This will help you get clarity on the objective for your game.

This can be difficult, because it involves defining what you want without the layers of others' expectations through which you have been conditioned to view your life and make your choices. I recommend starting with the extremes to help you gain clarity. For example, what were the things you wrote down that made you think, *No way, no how, I definitely don't want that for myself*? What were the things that made you think, *Yes, I must have that*? What made you react viscerally? Write it down in this worksheet.

By now you should be getting a good idea of the things that you do and don't want, even without the external validation of others and the layers of others' expectations placed on you. But let's go even further. Let's think about what brings you joy and makes you feel like a winner even when no one is watching.

Remember when you were a kid and you stole a cookie from the proverbial cookie jar without getting caught—and you felt like you got away with something and that you were clever and smart? Remember that nobody even needed to know that you ate the cookie because you did it just for you? What gets you feeling that way?

What makes you feel the way I feel at work when everybody's stressed and asking me if I'm gunning for the next promotion, and I just smile inside because I know that what I'm really gunning for is a monthlong project in Tokyo, the ability to work from the beach in Uruguay, teaching a class in Vietnam and swinging through Hong Kong on my way home, or figuring out a good excuse to go to South Africa?

What makes you feel like you're winning? What makes you so happy that you don't even care if other people know about it? That's a good thing to put at the heart of the objective of your game! For me, it's travel. For you, it might be more free time, or health and fitness goals, or seeing your kids thriving and happy. It may be starting a company or a nonprofit to help others in your community, or perhaps it's related to launching an online store to sell your macramé wall hangings that you love to make. Whatever it is, write it down.

WHAT MAKES YOU
HAPPY! HAPPY! HAPPY!
(even when no one else knows about it)?

Now . . . I get it. There are always trade-offs. I'm not going to sit here and tell you to throw everything away, quit your job, and chase your dream of finger-painting abstract art because that's what you love and what makes you happy. After all, if you spend all of your time finger-painting, it could mean you will struggle to buy food and pay bills and keep a roof over your head. But if your happiness comes from finger-painting, then arrange the more practical aspects of your life to maximize the amount of time available for painting. Get the shorter commute. Pay your bills with a job that gives you time to paint. Find friends and be in relationships with people who will support your desire to finger-paint and who will help you become the artist you feel you are inside.

After going through the exercises in the previous worksheets, take note of what *you* want for *you*, and write it down here.

WHAT DO YOU WANT?	WHY?

Again . . . I get it. There are bills to pay. There are other people to think about. It's not about only you as an individual. And often your objective involves other people in one way or another, so include others in your objective if that's important for you.

Remember that if you know what your objective is, you can make decisions and choices along the way to help you get there. And every year it's easier to shed others' expectations, get your game going, and win. It's a process, not a leap. But the one thing I will tell you with absolute certainty is that you'll never get there if you're always playing someone else's game.

> It's a process, not a leap. But the one thing I will tell you with absolute certainty is that you'll never get there if you're always playing someone else's game.

Now that you've had some time to think about it, what's the objective for your game? Write it down here.

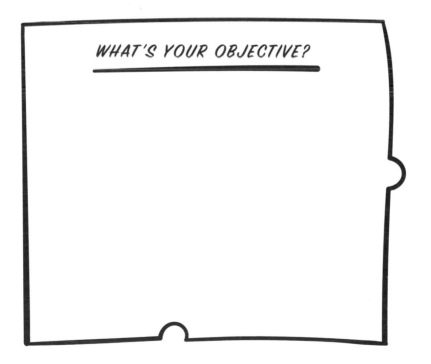

WHAT'S YOUR OBJECTIVE?

How Will You Play Your Game?

Now it's time to determine how you will play your game. What are the ways you will need to use your time, talent, and resources to play and win?

This is obviously very dependent on your objective and the game you want to play. Is it about where you spend your time? Or how you use your talents to achieve some other goal? In this part, think about what would have to happen for you to obtain your objective and win your game.

For my game of spending the most time in the coolest places, I chose to achieve my objective through work, so it meant that I spent time working in various roles as my means to an end. What are your means to your end? If your game's objective is to finger-paint, what needs to happen to be able to maximize your painting time? How do you need to spend your time and how do you need to adjust how you're currently spending your time in order to reach your objective?

Remember to include time for yourself each day as well as time for work and others. To play your game, you're going to need to have time to reflect, think, dream, and rest, so include those in your plan on how you'll spend your time. Also, think about how much sleep you really need (which may be more than what you're getting), when you'll make sure you're having some fun, and how you'll connect with those who are important to you. And don't forget time for exercising and eating well because those things are crucial for your health. Write it all down in the worksheet.

HOW DO YOU NEED TO SPEND YOUR TIME?

6 AM _____

_____

_____

_____

_____

_____

_____

_____

_____

_____

_____

2 AM _____

Now I want you to consider your talents. What talents do you have that you can use to play your game? Many of us focus on talents that we lack instead of recognizing the ones we already have. Make sure you think through both what you already have and what you need. What do you already have? What new skills do you need to develop, and how can you do this? What do you need to learn and how are you going to learn it? For example, do you already know how to finger-paint, or do you need to take a class?

WHAT TALENTS AND SKILLS DO YOU ALREADY HAVE?

WHAT TALENTS AND SKILLS WILL YOU NEED TO DEVELOP? HOW?

Finally, let's talk about resources. What resources do you need to be able to play your game? Where can you find them? Remember, money isn't the only resource out there! Other resources include time, talents and skills, and support from others.

For example, if your objective is to commit to doing five marathons each year because you love how you feel training and doing them, what resources will you need to find the time to train? Where can you find support in the form of a training buddy who will meet you in the park at 5 a.m. to go run 10 miles before work? Which friends will be supportive by not keeping you out late the night before because they know you need to wake up at 4:30 a.m. to train? Those examples are not about money, but they certainly are about other kinds of resources you might need.

If your objective is to provide a better life for your children, and you've determined that this will require you to enter a new industry that leads to better wages and opportunities than the work you're doing now, the resources you'll need likely have to do with new skills. Perhaps this means taking online classes on coding or software. Perhaps this means reading new websites and journals or watching videos of experts in that field. Perhaps it means making a friend in that industry and taking them for coffee or for a walk in the park to learn from them. You will play your game by doing these things.

Or maybe your objective is to open your own restaurant. What resources will you need to do this? Maybe you'll need to take cooking classes or work in someone else's restaurant to learn the ins and outs of the business. Maybe you'll need help from a knowledgeable friend to choose the right location.

Maybe you'll need some help marketing to nearby neighbor-hoods and businesses.

What resources will you need to acquire for your game? And how can you obtain them? Write it down in the worksheet. And who knows—you might already have some of them, like musical or artistic talent or an ability to run fast or a love of learning or the ability to speak several languages. Whatever it is, write it down.

> **WHAT RESOURCES DO YOU ALREADY HAVE?**
>
> **WHAT WILL YOU NEED TO FIND? HOW?**

Now let's put it together. Write down your objective from the previous section again in the puzzle piece labeled "What is the objective?" below, and in the box labeled "How do you play?" list the ways you will spend your time and resources that you already have in the pursuit of your game's objective. You can also make a note of the things you need to acquire in order to play your game.

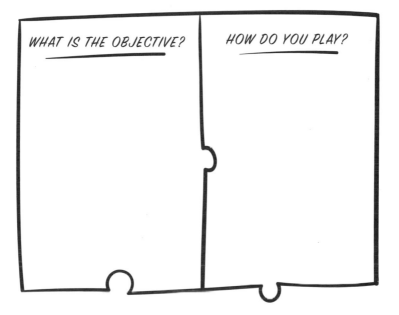

What Obstacles Must You Overcome?

Now let's work on the third step in the game. As you know, all games have challenges. Whether it's the opposing team in a basketball game or the luck of the draw in solitaire, challenges are what create opportunities for you to use your wit and skills to find a way to win regardless of the obstacles.

Obstacles can come in many varieties, from your own fears that hold you back to people who are trying to bring you down. Understanding the obstacles you'll face will help you know what kinds of resilience you'll

Challenges are what create opportunities for you to use your wit and skills to find a way to win regardless of the obstacles.

need to develop and what kinds of support you'll require in order to ultimately prevail and win your game.

One of my favorite posts, attributed to walkingmyhellhound, on boardofwisdom.com says, "If I've learned anything from video games, it is that when you meet enemies, it means that you are going in the right direction." Winning isn't always easy, and you will encounter obstacles. But like in a video game, with the right tools and skills and support, you can reach the goal.

Finding the Right Kind of Support

Although it's sometimes difficult to admit, one of the biggest obstacles can be lack of the right kind of support from those around us. As I touched on in chapter 4, the right kind of support is key to thriving and being successful in your game, but it's not always easy because often those around us are supportive when we are doing what is expected of us, but they are not necessarily supportive when we are trying to change.

In an effort to understand if finding the right kind of support is an obstacle for you, dig deeper and ask yourself which people are holding you back right now and which people are trying to rein you in. Often this happens out of someone's own insecurities and fears that they project onto you, or it happens because they have selfish interests in your fulfillment of expectations related to them. In effect, those people may be keeping you down and dimming your light. Remember this, as those may not be people you can draw on for the right kind of support as you start to change your game.

Ask yourself who the people are who simply wanted to help you be who you wanted to be. Who were the teachers, coaches, neighbors, crazy aunties, colleagues, and other people who were there to support you wholly without judgment and without control? Who were the people who were cheering you on when you were doing something ridiculous that you enjoyed immensely? Remember these people, because they are likely to be the people you'll want to call on for support in your new game. And you'll probably want to look for more people like these in your life to support you as you start playing your own game.

Remember: There's no judgment here. There have been moments in my life where I realized I was not surrounded by supportive people. Instead, I was surrounded by people who wanted something from me. They wanted my time, my resources, my talents, or access to people I knew. I was surrounded by people who were trying to hold me down and hold me back for their own reasons. I was spending my time trying to convince people who were not supportive of me that I was worthy of their support. I tried to be more of what they wanted me to be, I tried to please them, and I tried to play their game.

And then at some point I realized there are *7 billion people* on the planet and that surely a few of them would support me rather than hold me back. This was a truly humbling moment for me, because I realized that I had been choosing to surround myself with unsupportive people, and I was trying very hard to get them to support me—and that was never going to happen. Eventually I realized that a better use of my energy would be to look for new people in my life. I realized that I wanted to look for people who would be supportive in the ways that I needed support. And it took a long time (like, years) and a lot of effort to find myself surrounded by people who supported me in my game rather than by people who were detractors.

Every now and then, I look at the people in my life and I evaluate who's supporting me and who's holding me back, and I adjust who I spend my time with accordingly. My closest friends who know this are always happy that they make the cut! What they don't realize is how grateful I am that I make their cut as well.

Who are the people supporting you in the ways you need to be supported? Go find more of them. And for those who are not so supportive, spend less of your time and energy on them. Spend your energy finding people who already do. They're out there.

Pause and consider the important people in your life. Who are the people supporting you in the ways you need to be supported? Make a list of those people and go find more of them. And for those who are not so supportive, spend less of your time and energy on them. Stop trying to convince them to support you. Instead, spend your energy finding people who already do. They're out there. It just takes time to figure out who's who, because the first people to pop up in your life are often those who want something from you.

You've got to wade through the mishmash first and then find your supporters. And know that there are always those people who are in the gray area. You think they support you, but somehow you're not really sure. And you're not sure if they'd support you changing your game to be more in line with what's right for you. Maybe those people are not supporting you in the ways you need to be supported. Perhaps you can ask them to support you in the ways that you need and then see how it goes.

Learning Something New

As part of playing my game of "Spending the Most Amount of Time in the Coolest Places," I knew I'd need to continuously develop business and technology skills desired by global companies, but I also knew that I would need to learn a language. And Spanish was particularly relevant to the organization with which I was working at the time. I needed to become fluent enough to conduct business in Spanish, which is a whole different level of fluency than *"Dónde está la biblioteca?"* I also knew that I did not have a natural affinity for learning languages or for pronunciation because before trying to learn Spanish, I had studied French in high school and could sort of read a menu. I studied one year of Russian in college and could kind of remember the sounds of the Cyrillic alphabet letters. However, if you had sent me to France or to Russia, my language skills would have been woefully inadequate. But I needed to learn, so I started taking classes at a program that was world renowned as the best. And it was awful.

I didn't understand anything. The instructor just looked at me and yelled words I didn't know and expected me to respond, thinking apparently that just yelling at me would somehow imprint the words in my brain and magically I'd begin to speak beautiful Spanish. I tried another teacher who wanted me to do tons of worksheets with tons of verb conjugations so I got some grammar down, but I couldn't speak to anyone. I mean, how often do you use "I go, he goes, we go, you go, they go" in a conversation? Clearly frustration was setting in, and I was feeling stupid—and like I'd never learn.

People referred me to different programs, and I found one that combined listening, written exercises, and talking on the phone to the teacher. Not only was this great because it meant I could speak to her from anywhere, but also it was great because she magically tailored our conversations to my level of Spanish so that I didn't feel stupid. She was kind and gently corrected me when I said something wrong, and she helped me build up my confidence by basically forcing me to carry out 30- and 60-minute long conversations *only* in Spanish—from the beginner level all the way through to advanced. Now, I imagine this must have been such a lesson in patience for her, and some days I think about how slowly she must have had to speak at first for me to grasp the most basic of concepts; but it was great for me because it helped me learn in a way that made sense to me, and it also helped me build confidence, which I had been lacking, given the styles of other language programs I'd tried.

Mostly I share this story because it's an example of knowing that I needed to learn Spanish and that in order to learn, I'd need to feel confident. I needed to find support and the right kind of program for me, and only then would I be ready—with knowledge and confidence—to put myself out there and speak in Spanish in meetings. When I first started speaking Spanish in the office, people would often look at me with their eyes open wide, then kind of look down toward the floor. I figured I must have said something completely incomprehensible or extremely profane. But other times people would smile and be patient and help me along until I reached a level of fluency where they stopped taking it easy on me. That base of preparation was important for building my confidence, and it's part of my process. Many people wouldn't characterize me as cautious, but those who really know me know that there's always a preparation going on underneath the surface. In fact, my dad often says that I'm like a duck—it all looks smooth on top of the water, but underneath I'm paddling like hell. Remember to reflect on what things you need to learn to play your game and how are you going to learn them.

Taking an Approach That Works for You

As I mentioned in the example about Spanish, finding the approach that works best for you is key whenever you're making a change or doing something new. As I've gotten more honest with myself over time, I have realized that judgment and criticism really shut me down. So whenever I'm doing something new, I tend to be very careful with myself, especially in the beginning, to avoid criticism and judgment. I cushion myself while building up my confidence by reaching out to those I know will support me, by looking for other kinds of support, and by avoiding people I know are not supportive and who fly out with criticisms on a regular basis. Basically I give myself some incubation time before I let my idea out into the world because I know I need to be cautious with myself.

I've also had to deal with obstacles related to disappointment, and deal with haters. In fact, these obstacles never disappear completely. But with time, I seem to get better at managing them because I've developed resilience, overcome some fears, and continue to evolve and grow. You may also need to put some strategies in place that work for you to deal with similar obstacles that arise.

And maybe as you become more aware about how you approach something new, you'll discover you are like me in that you need to be cautious and feel prepared and competent when launching into something new. Or maybe you are comfortable being more reckless, and if that works for you, that's great. But if you need to be more cautious with yourself like I do, that's OK too. Just know what works for you. Be honest with yourself about it and act accordingly.

How Will You Overcome Your Obstacles?

Obviously overcoming the obstacles that you'll need to overcome to play your new game isn't necessarily going to be quick and easy. You are likely to encounter obstacles that require longterm commitments. After all, you don't become fluent in a new language in a day. But that's the whole point. This is your game for the long haul, so you should expect to be making long-term investments to be able to win.

So go ahead and reflect and take a shot at naming your obstacles and think about how to overcome them. Perhaps your obstacles have to do with finding time to pursue a hobby.

Perhaps one way to overcome this obstacle is to cook all of your meals on Sunday and put them in the freezer so that during the week, you have time for your hobby because you don't have to cook. Maybe you need guidance on training for that marathon because you had a knee injury, so you need to consult experts who can help you strengthen your muscles so you can train without doing more damage to yourself. Or maybe you need to take a second job or earn some additional income to save for that around-the-world trip you've been dreaming of.

I'm not being flippant or saying this stuff is easy, but I *am* saying that it's possible if you're focused on your objective and on getting the right resources and support in place that you'll need to play your game. I worked during both college and grad school, often 30–40 hours a week. And for four years, I had both a corporate job and a university job, which meant I was working six to seven days a week without holidays during that time.

Whatever they may be, take time to name the obstacles that are getting in your way and consider ways to overcome them.

WHAT OBSTACLES WILL YOU FACE?	HOW WILL YOU OVERCOME THEM?
SUPPORT	
LEARNING NEW THINGS	
FINDING TIME	
WHAT ELSE?	

Don't Ignore the Deeper Internal Obstacles

Now, the obstacles that I mentioned above are all real, but by making clever choices about the way your game is played, they can be overcome. Sometimes the biggest, most difficult obstacles touch on our own deeper, internal fears and insecurities. We all have them—yes, even the people who seem to be living fabulous lives. It's OK to have fears and insecurities, and sometimes naming and recognizing them actually helps us stop them from getting in the way. Here are some of the most common fears:

FEAR OF FAILURE

It seems obvious that when you're discovering and designing your own game, sometimes you worry about whether or not you'll succeed. What if you don't finish the marathon? Or find a new job in a new industry? What if you move to a new city and it's just not the right place for you? What if you fall flat on your face in whatever new endeavor you've defined as your objective? These fears can really get your brain freaking out, and because of those fears, your brain may seek comfort and keep you in your status quo. But if you move your thinking to your frontal lobe, you'll realize that failure is a part of life.

I've failed repeatedly in both public and private ways. It's not fun. It hurts. It's humbling. But at least I know I'm trying. At least I'm participating. At least I'm moving forward. And to be honest, most of the time the failures loomed larger in my own head than they seemed to anybody else. In fact, some of the things that I consider to be my most spectacular failures nobody else even noticed or remembers. These include a short-lived stand-up comedy career, a dismal presentation at a professional conference that left me in tears in front of the audience, embarrassing amounts of desperation in one particular romantic relationship, various and pitiful attempts at team sports at all ages, and almost flunking out of a graduate school program.

FEAR OF SUCCESS

Some people may think this is strange, but a fear of success does exist. What if you achieve the thing you've been working so hard for and you're still not happy or satisfied? What if you spend all of this energy and realize you were focused on the wrong thing? This is no reason not to try. You may not get your objective quite right the first time, but that's why you can continue to refine and change your game as you get to know yourself better and you understand what does and doesn't make you happy. Sometimes we have to go through the steps of pursuing something and then finding out it's not what we really wanted in order to figure out what we really do want. For me, this has taken many years and continues to evolve.

OTHERS LAUGHING AT YOU

This is a big one and it definitely triggers your amygdala and makes you feel profoundly unsafe. I know many people who don't want to take risks or try something new because they're afraid that others will laugh at them. And people might. But again, if we move to the frontal lobe, you realize that at least you're doing something with your life. At least you're participating and trying and growing and blossoming as a human being, whereas the people laughing at you are stuck in the same place, judging others instead of seeing how they can improve themselves.

If you find yourself with this fear, my recommendation is

to go slowly, find other people who will be supportive of your new endeavor, and spend time with them so that by the time you start playing your game, you have supporters around you rather than detractors. Remember, this is a long-term game, so everything doesn't have to happen quickly or all at once. Take the time to get your support in place, so your support group's cheers will drown out anyone else's laughter. Remember, change is always easier with supportive people around you.

SOMETHING BAD HAPPENING

This is my own personal fear. Perhaps I inherited it from family members who fear change and immediately imagine the worst and most extreme situations that could possibly occur. Talk about your brain freaking out! Seriously. I used to say that my mom should have been a cowriter with Stephen King because her imagination can turn the most mundane situation into something horrific.

Over time, I have found that by saying the hypothetical bad thing out loud, it immediately becomes smaller and more manageable. I also started personifying bad things that could happen as cute little cartoon monsters, and they stopped being so big and scary. If this is your particular fear, perhaps you could spend some time doing prework to find a way to manage your own little monsters that may be getting in the way of playing your own game.

Don't be afraid to name your fears and deal with your internal obstacles. Remember you don't have to dive into

Don't be afraid to name your fears and deal with your internal obstacles.

something before you're ready, but don't just stand there. Do the hard work you need to do in order to *get* yourself ready, and then go for it. Write down your *real* obstacles here. Get them out in the open so you can face them and get through them.

WHAT ARE THE REAL OBSTACLES
YOU NEED TO OVERCOME?
HOW WILL YOU DO IT?

Now it's time to put these three pieces of your game together. You know your objective, you know how to play your game, and you know the obstacles that you'll face and overcome. Go ahead and write those three pieces of your game down here!

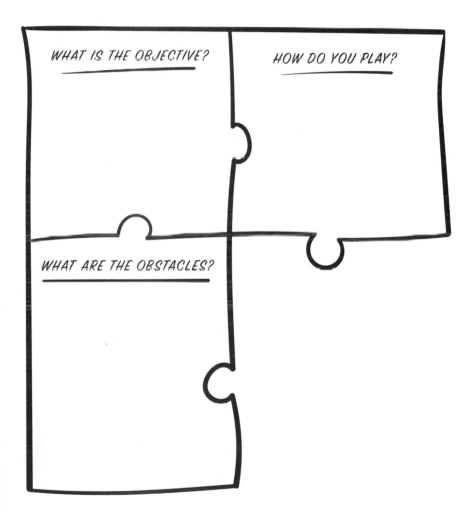

There's just one more piece that needs to be defined.

How Will You Keep Score and Know That You're Winning?

This part should be fun! You should have some engaging, visual way to help you see when you are scoring points and to help you know that you're winning. Whether it's an annual calendar of your trips or a studio space in your home where you display your finger paintings, you need a scoreboard that shows your progress and that's evidence that you're winning!

What will your scoreboard look like?

WHAT'S YOUR SCOREBOARD?

• • •

Obviously, it's now time to put all of the pieces together. Take the work you've done so far and put it all in one place in the following figure so you can keep turning back to it, especially when you find yourself getting discouraged or off track.

Fill out all of the pieces of your new game.

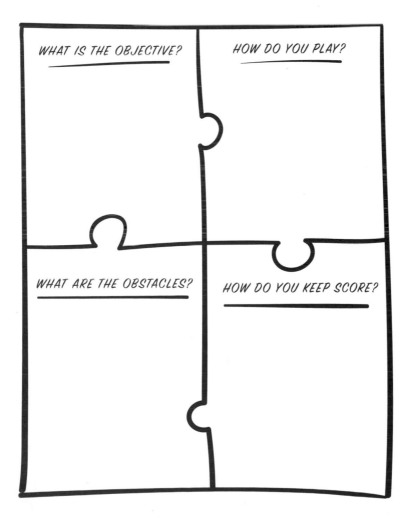

Now sit back, smile, and congratulate yourself for taking a huge step forward toward redefining your success and achieving what matters most.

REMEMBER:

- Reflect and unravel your conditioning and others' expectations to be able to construct an objective that is important, meaningful, and inspiring to you.
- Be intentional in how you play your game and in how you use your time, talent, and resources each day in pursuit of your objective.
- The obstacles are real, especially the internal ones. Work on those so you can play your game from a position of strength and confidence.
- Keep score, kick butt, and win.

CHAPTER 7

Making It Happen

Moving from the game you're playing now to a new game can be difficult. This change can be hard because even if you're ready for it, those around you will have a reaction to your shifts in behavior, in objectives, and in how you choose to spend your time, talent, and resources. Sometimes it can feel like you're waging a scorched-earth campaign or like you're starting an earthquake when you transition from playing an old game to playing a new one.

Start Small

My recommendation is to start small. Start with little things that feel good to you and that help others see that there's been a shift in your behavior and in what you will and won't do. This will not only allow you to get ready for bigger changes, but it will ease those around you in to these changes as well. Starting small is a

> **Start with little things that feel good to you and that help others see that there's been a shift in your behavior and in what you will and won't do.**

benefit because, if you will remember from chapter 3, when you do things that others don't expect, both their brains and your brain might have little freak-outs. It's good to start small so that you and those around you can get used to the idea that some things will be changing. You can build up some small successes and then have the courage and confidence to tackle bigger personal, professional, and life games.

Here are some small games I've played at different points in my life, just to give you some ideas to get going:

- The game of "Not Getting Stuck with the Action Items in a Meeting"
- The game of "Not Touching PowerPoint for Three Months"
- The game of "Never Starting Meetings before 10 a.m. or Ending Them after 4 p.m."
- The game of "Scheduling Classes Only for Tuesdays and Thursdays"
- The game of "Having My Nails Done Once a Week"
- The game of "Having My Handbag and Shoes Match Each Day"

The more you play these small games, the more comfortable you will become with making changes in your life and then the easier it will be to start playing bigger games.

What You Need to Start Making Changes

As mentioned previously, making changes is difficult. Other people might tell you it's easy and to just do it. However, given conditioning and the way our brains and other people's brains react to change, it can be scary and filled with uncertainty. And it can also be exhilarating and joyful once you've made the changes. My experiences have shown me that approaching changes with your eyes open about what you are doing, why, what kinds of challenges you may face, and how you'll handle them if or when they arise are all key. So what will you need to make the changes?

- **Courage.** Change brings uncertainty, and so the fear of the unknown often makes the status quo look preferable. You, your amygdala, and others in your life may want to pull you backward to the status quo. Be emboldened and go forward instead.

- **Vision.** What would be better than your status quo? This is not a "grass is greener/get a new sofa" kind of change but a real shift in *how* you spend your time, talent, and resources as well as a shift in *why* you spend them that way. Can you envision a future where your efforts are going toward those things that matter most to you?

- **Support**. Actual emotional and practical support—not fake, self-serving, or self-interested support—from people who believe in you, who want you to do great, and who aren't insecure or competing with you.

- **Your game plan.** Which you're designing in this book.

Whenever anyone asks me about change, I think back to the changes over the course of my life. I've experienced several pretty monumental, cataclysmic shifts, and I've used some pretty tough tactics to push myself past the points of pain that come with change and to help me break through to the other side.

One example was when I knew I needed to make a big shift in my life. I had been living in Argentina, married, and working for a large telecommunications company. Over a period of about six months, I found myself moving back to the US, no longer married, and with no job, as the company I had been working for was sold to another company who did not want me on their payroll. I owned a beautiful, expensive loft that happened to be underwater because the housing market was stalling. I had some savings but way more debt, and I was suffering from a broken heart that was longing to live anywhere except in the loft I'd shared with my ex-husband.

Eventually I received a job offer from a consulting firm, which was great news, and they wanted me to live in the US and work for their domestic telecommunications practice, which was not such great news. I wanted to work internationally; and even though I had no other options, I called them and told them I didn't want the job. My brain was freaking out and it was really scary, but I needed to cut off that option in order to push myself to look for something new in line with what I did want. A few months later, I received an offer to move back to Argentina, earning devaluing pesos rather than dollars, and I took it. I used the rest of my savings to get out of my upside-down mortgage, I moved again to Argentina, and I never looked back.

Whenever people ask me about that time in my life and those choices, I explain that it came down to a realization that if I worked for a consulting firm in the US, inevitably there would be a Friday night where I would be snowed in at an airport somewhere trying to get home, and I'd likely be thinking, "I could be in Argentina right now." But there would never be a moment in Argentina where I would be thinking, "I could be snowed in on a Friday night in an airport right now." Not that Argentina is perfect. It's definitely not. But I needed to push myself back in that direction to continue on my journey of playing my game. It was drastic and although it was not impossible, it was really hard and not a safe choice at all.

One evening in a bar in Hong Kong, a perfect stranger was eavesdropping on my conversation with a friend while I was telling her about that time of change and upheaval in my life. Mr. Perfect Stranger inserted himself into the conversation to tell me that not all changes have to be so dramatic and disruptive and that everything doesn't have to get thrown up in the air when making changes in life. He reminded me that changes can be more progressive and planned than that.

And he was right. You can make plans, but make them and then act on them. Do the things that you need to do to push yourself to act. Set your alarm clock earlier. Sign up and actually go to a class or training. Make the extra calls. Cut off all your other options if that's what works for you. The truth is, you know when you're procrastinating or avoiding out of fear or uncertainty. Work with yourself to figure

Do the things that you need to do to push yourself to act.

out the best way to make you act on your plan. Work with your-self to make you do the things you know you need to do. Like when it's time to let go of something (like a relationship) or fix something (like having a big surgery you've been putting off) or look for a new job (because you're miserable).

You know when you need to make changes and act, because you can feel the tectonic plates starting to shift underneath your surface. It may not be apparent to others and they may not even notice, but you feel the subtle shifts. And eventually the pressure comes to the top and the change occurs. There may be an earth-quake, hopefully mild, and some aftershocks, hopefully small, but after the change you'll wonder, *Why the hell didn't I do it sooner? Why was I waiting so long to make the change?*

Is change hard? You bet it is! People make it look easy, but they rarely tell you about their struggles along the way. People usually tell the story after the change has occurred, after the dust has settled, and when they're finally feeling confident about their new direction. They rarely talk about the tough moments in the beginning and the middle. Maybe it's because it's eas-ier to explain the story and connect the dots looking backward (thanks, Steve Jobs, for that graduation speech).[1] Or maybe it's more difficult to talk about changes when you're in the middle of the storm trying to figure out which way to go. Or maybe it's because you just don't want to have to justify it to other people.

---

1   For Jobs's graduation address to Stanford, see "'You've Got to Find What You Love' Jobs Says", *Stanford News*, June 14, 2005.

Some Strategies to Push Yourself

In case it's useful, here are my strategies for pushing forward with changes that aren't easy. Often, I'll write a letter to my "new" self reminding me how unhappy my "old" self was, just in case I ever start getting nostalgic and my memory plays tricks on me about how great the past was, which can happen when you're in the midst of a change and feeling uncomfortable. I also find it helpful to close my eyes and picture myself five years from now driving a car, which for me represents where I'm going and what's ahead in my life. Where am I driving? What kind of car is it? Where am I coming from and where am I going? Who's in the car with me? Those kinds of questions help me stay in touch with what I want for my life and help me get through difficult periods when I'm on the road to a new game. You may have your own strategies or you may find these helpful. Whatever works for you, embrace it.

For what it's worth, in this phase of my life, I'm trying out the path of making changes that are more progressive, with smaller steps that are less chaotic and dramatic. I'm trying to take Mr. Perfect Stranger's advice. So far, so good. It takes longer, and sometimes I find that I'm impatient with this new approach; but again, the big life game is a marathon, not a sprint. And it's my game. So it's my choice how fast or slow I want to play it.

Rule 1 (and the only rule there is): It's your game and you get to make the rules and play it however you want.

Rule 1 (and the only rule there is): It's your game and you get to make the rules and play it however you want.

In the next chapter, we'll look at some ways to actually apply this framework and these lessons to your life.

REMEMBER:

- Start small to get yourself and others comfortable with changes, be kind to yourself during the process, and go at your own pace. But go. Don't stand still. Go.

CHAPTER 8

Playing Games, Big and Small

Because redefining success and designing your new game can be difficult the first time you do it, here are a few examples to illustrate how you can incorporate games both big and small into your life. First, we'll look at a silly one and then we'll look at some examples of games that can make a bigger impact on your life.

Playing the Game of "Not Eating Lunch at Your Desk"

To start, let's say you're tired of eating lunch at your desk while you're busily typing away at emails and answering phones. You know that sitting is the new smoking, that it's bad for your health, that your posture suffers, and you just don't like it and you're a bit resentful that the culture in your office has resulted in this state of things.

So you decide to play a new game. Instead of playing the game your company culture has conditioned you to play of "Scarfing Down Food as Fast as Possible to Be Able to Cram in More Work

and Emails," you're going to design and play your own game based
on *not* eating lunch at your desk. How will this work?

What is the objective of your game?

Being the person in your office who leaves the building to eat
lunch out the most often.

How do you play your game?

You get up and walk out of the building to eat lunch for 30–60
minutes (or more!).

What are the obstacles?

Your boss who dumps work on your desk at noon each day. The
lady in accounting who disappears every day for an hour and a
half and nobody knows where she goes, but she currently wins
the "Who Leaves the Office the Most" game. Your coworkers
who are glued to their desks all day long. Your fear that if your
boss sees you not working for those 30 minutes, there will be
consequences, and your brain probably starts freaking out about
the potential repercussions.

These are all reasonable obstacles, so it's time to use your wits
to figure out how to get around them to be able to win your game:

- Why not leave your desk at 11:45 a.m. to get your lunch so
  you miss your boss's noon request? If you return at 12:30 p.m.

and receive the request then, there's not likely to be much of a difference.

- Why not follow the lady from accounting to see what she's doing? Maybe she's napping in her car (and winning her own game!), or maybe she could become an ally and supporter of you in your quest to win your game.

- Why not enlist your colleagues to start forging a new culture of eating lunch away from your desk? After all, there's power in numbers, and I'm sure you're not the only one who dislikes eating lunch at a desk.

- Why not speak with your boss and explain that studies show your productivity goes up when you take breaks? And then show that to be the case with great performance.

How do you keep score and know you're winning?

Remember that this is your game, so you make the rules about the score, what counts, and what doesn't. For example, does eating your lunch in the parking lot count as "out"? Does it count if you're gone fewer than 30 minutes? Your game. Your rules.

You can put up a scoreboard at your desk that tracks three to four of your colleagues and you regarding daily lunch habits for the week, and you can mark a "check" each time you or one of them goes out to lunch. The one with the most checks that week wins. Super simple. Super easy.

Here's what it could look like.

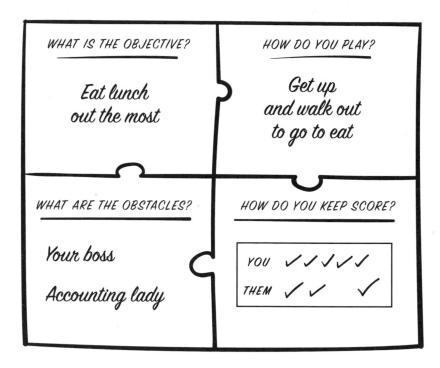

Again, this is a silly little example, it's a way you can take something that annoys you, like eating lunch at your desk, and turn it into something you can be a little mischievous with and have a sense of winning. And by the way, just getting away from your desk will have good benefits for your health, energy, and sanity, which will help with your attitude and relationships with your friends, loved ones, and yourself. So maybe it's not such a silly little example after all.

Playing the Game of "Getting More Joy in Your Life"

Now let's try a slightly bigger example, and this one is real for me. For many years, I had chronic pain that was debilitating and limited me from doing many different kinds of physical activities. After a surgery solved the issue, I was able to work out and enjoy physical activity again. This was truly a gift, and I was super grateful to feel good again. I realized that having good health and being physically fit were gifts, and as such, I needed to *enjoy* them more.

So I looked back on my life and remembered that some of the moments that were filled with pure joy for me were when I was a teenager playing around on a surfboard on the beach near where I grew up. I was never good at surfing, and the waves on the beach in my small town in Florida never got above two or three feet, so it's not like there was massive shredding of waves going on. Nevertheless, playing around on the board in the waves was truly joyful for me, and the feeling of catching a wave, when all of Mother Nature lifts you up on that board, was one of the most amazing things I've ever experienced.

So I set out to bring more joy in my life by starting to surf again. Here's what that game looked like for me.

What is the objective of your game?

Bring joy into my life through surfing as a way to celebrate my ability to do fun physical activities again.

How do you play your game?

Take trips to places with waves, rent a board, paddle out, try to catch waves—sometimes actually catching them and riding them all the way to the shore, sometimes getting knocked off the board and tossed around. And then get up, laugh and smile, and do it all over again.

What are the obstacles?

There have been many! First and foremost, I had to recover from my surgery and get myself in good enough shape to be able to paddle out, pop up, stay balanced on the board, and overcome the fear that inevitably arises when you get knocked off the board and tossed around by a wave like you're in a washing machine and don't know which way is up. So what did I do?

I started working on my fitness. I knew that surfing would be no fun if my fitness level wasn't up to snuff, so I focused on core stability in the gym. This included tons of work on my abdominals but it also included work on my arms for paddling out, burpees for pop ups, and lots of lower-body strength to be able to balance on the board.

Once I felt strong, I moved to more challenging balance work—like standing on my knees on a ball and using a balance board to improve my side-to-side stability. My trainer and I worked together and he would throw medicine balls at me while I was trying to stay upright on these unstable surfaces in order to force me to get used to maintaining my balance even while he was intentionally trying to throw me off.

Then I discovered an exercise class where you actually do exercises *on a surfboard*! It mimics instability and forces your stabilizer muscles to work, and the classes focus on the muscles you use when surfing.

Now, I don't always love the gym or exercise classes, but knowing that I was doing this to eventually engage in an activity that was pure joy for me made it easier and something I actually looked forward to and was willing to schedule my nights and weekends around.

Second, I had to face the fact that I live in a landlocked city. There is no surfing where I live, which means I'd have to travel to be able to have that joy. I started researching surfing locations that were within driving distance or just a short, cheap flight away. I started planning vacations around surfing and I have surfed in places like Florida, Costa Rica, Mexico, and Puerto Rico.

Finally, I had to face up to some fears. The first big one for me was the fear of failure. What if I couldn't catch a wave? Or was just really bad at surfing? What if other people saw how bad I surfed? My brain freaked out and my fears about others laughing at me needed to be dealt with. So I reminded myself that I wasn't doing this to compete with others or to be better than anybody else or even to be particularly good at all for that matter. I was doing this just for joy and to celebrate the fact that my body can engage in this type of activity and be filled by the rhythm of the ocean and the waves.

The other big fear was related to my own physical safety and the safety of those around me. What if I got pulled under by a wave and didn't know which way was up and kind of started running out of air, which sometimes happens? What if I accidentally ran over another surfer in the water because of my inability to handle the board? What if I got run over by somebody else? In order for me to enjoy surfing, I had to minimize these fears and my brain freak-outs. This meant—you guessed it—more time in the gym to ensure my strength and ability to handle the board. But it also meant making a deal with myself that I'd always and only surf with an instructor who was from the local area, who knew the waves and riptides and currents, and who would look out for me and others ... just in case.

With plans in place to overcome those obstacles, I felt like I was in a good place to start this game!

How do you keep score and know you're winning?

This was easy for me. It was simply answering these questions: How many times over the course of a year could I get to a beach and surf? And how many times a week was I taking a class or working out in the gym to get prepared to surf? I do not measure how many waves I catch, how big they are, if I am any good, or even if I'm getting any better. I just measure the amount of time I'm giving myself to pursue joy.

Here's what it looks like using our framework.

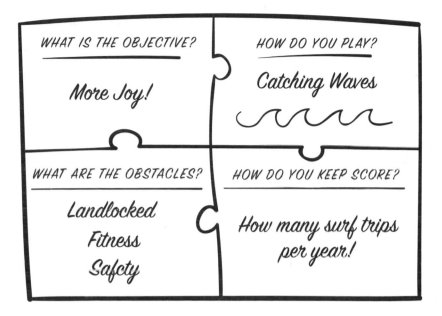

Playing the Game of "Changing Careers"

Going out for lunch and finding your joy through surfing are great examples of playing your game. Let's take a final example that goes deeper into fundamental life changes, and this one involves a career shift.

When I was in college, I asked myself the usual question: "What do I want to do with my life?" I had planned to go to law school not out of passion but because I didn't know what else to do and it seemed like a reasonable next step. My boyfriend in college was also applying to law schools. It was really important to him to get into a good school and I knew that there would be relationship stress during my senior year of college if we were both trying to get into the same competitive schools.

So I pivoted and decided to seek out other kinds of graduate programs instead.

I applied to PhD programs in international politics and economics, thinking that I would eventually work in the policy arena or teach at the university level. I was accepted to a program and during that time, I worked for an NGO and also taught courses on the side at a university. I finished my PhD and was slated to go on the academic job market, and in the process of applying for jobs, I realized this path was no longer right for me. Through the PhD program, I learned that I wasn't passionate about research and although my students were great, teaching had left me kind of bored. It became clear that even though I'd invested nine years of my adult life in higher education, not to mention unimaginable mental, financial, and emotional resources, I knew I needed to leave and find something else. I was 27 years old, and was leaving all I had known. Trying to break into something new at that age felt impossible, dangerous, and foolish. My brain was freaking out and tried to convince me to follow the safe path and stay in academia, but I did not listen.

I was 27 years old, and was leaving all I had known. Trying to break into something new at that age felt impossible, dangerous, and foolish.

In retrospect, I was quite lost and I didn't know how to handle the situation. I had no business skills, no real contacts anywhere, and no confidence in my ability to make a change. But I knew I had to do something so I did the only thing I knew how to do—I cut off all of my options. I applied for zero academic positions. I did not renew an adjunct contract with the university where I'd been teaching. I applied to zero post-doctorate fellowships. I basically pulled the equivalent of a Cortez ship burning, when he had his crews burn their ships so there was no turning back, only going forward in their explorations of new worlds. I cut off all options and had no choice but to march forward into completely unknown territory. I was terrified.

I started thinking about my objective, which was to work in the business world. In my PhD program, I'd studied quite a bit of economics and decision sciences, which I thought would be relevant to big companies; and as you already know, I've always had an affinity and interest in different cultures and countries. So I set out to find a job in that arena. A job. Any job. Please. I was desperate.

So to use our framework, that game went something like this.

What is the objective?

Find a job in international business with a company where there would be long-term potential. Obviously I didn't want to be looking for a job again any time soon, as it was such a painful process for me.

How do you play?

Let's be honest. This was an awful time for me. Everything I'd geared my life up for professionally was being thrown out the window and I was marching into the unknown at my own prodding. Talk about my amygdala and my brain going nuts! I played this game with prayer, with tears, with nausea, and with fear.

And then I got focused, and played the hell out of it by figuring out the obstacles and tackling them one by one.

What are the obstacles?

The first obstacle I faced was that I had zero business experience. The second was that I had zero confidence. The third was that I had zero network to reach out to for help in the world outside of academia.

Recognizing the uphill battle I was fighting, I reached out for help and did what was probably the dumbest thing at the time and the smartest thing for the long haul. I hired a career consultant/resume writer. I found this person in an advertisement and paid them the equivalent of three months of my university salary, which was a huge expense for me. I figured that if other people had paid me to teach them stuff, maybe I should pay someone else to teach me how to do a job search and a career transition.

This person taught me how to write a resume, and more importantly, he taught me how to talk about transferable skills, which basically means he taught me to translate things I'd done in academia into words that were relevant to business people. So instead of talking about the research I did that produced an R-squared of 62 and was statistically significant at the .005 level, which was what academics wanted to hear, he taught me to translate that into work I'd done in coding, statistical analysis, research, report writing, presenting, and teamwork—all of which were more relevant to business people. He completely rewrote my whole life in a language that was more relevant to the business world, and I have used and reused those skills that he taught me a million times as I've made many transitions in functional areas, roles, geographies, and industries in my professional career.

After he redid my resume, he worked on my confidence. He taught me how to deliver my elevator speech, how to order the words in a way that was authentic but impactful to a person listening with a business lens, and how to write emails that would capture the attention of Human Resource teams based on his understanding of what they were looking for when recruiting.

Finally, he worked with me on my network. Again, I knew nobody in the business world, but it turned out that from my NGO work, I had the names of a lot of influential people in big companies due to their associations with the NGO.

Armed with my new resume, a little bit of confidence, and a list of names of people I did not know, I basically started cold-calling. I sent letters, I made follow-up calls, I sent emails, I invited people to coffee. I did everything I could so that my name would keep popping up at the organizations I had on my target list. In the company that finally hired me, I later found out that I had sent my resume to five or six executives and they all forwarded it to the same person—my hiring manager—so the hiring manager was like, "Wow, this person knows a lot of important people at this company, and they all are recommending her for my group. I need to speak with her!" Even though none of them knew me at all. But anyway . . . I ended up getting an offer. My career counselor helped me negotiate my salary, and I joined a company that I worked for happily for seven years.

How do you measure success?

Getting a job with people who seemed decent in an industry that was interesting to me, where I could work internationally, and where I grew with new kinds of roles and challenges over a period of seven years. Here's what that game looked like.

WHAT IS THE OBJECTIVE?	HOW DO YOU PLAY?
Career shift into an international business role	Get help from resume writer, cold call, meet people, persistence
WHAT ARE THE OBSTACLES?	**HOW DO YOU KEEP SCORE?**
Transferable skills No Confidence No Network	Landing a job I like in a good company with growth potential

No matter how big or how small the changes are that you need to make in your life, you can use these steps to make your life better. Identify what it is that's needing to change, and then redefine what success means to you in that area, design your game, and play it! Start with small things, and then use those same skills to tackle the bigger questions in the game of life.

REMEMBER:

- You can play games, big and small, to help you make changes and improvements in all areas of your life.

CHAPTER 9

What Games Are Other People Playing?

There are many games out there, big and small. Sometimes when I look around, I see people playing the "Make the Most Money" game and arranging their life around investment banking, 6 a.m. start times, and the occasional use of illicit substances to keep their energy up and their exhaustion at bay. I also see people playing the "Make Time for Me" game, organizing their work life to end by 3 p.m. so they can coach their kids' soccer teams or dive into a woodworking hobby.

Almost any type of lifestyle—or lifestyle goal—can be turned into a game. Here are just a few to inspire you.

The "Maximize the Free Time" Game

One person I know plays the "Maximize the Free Time" game, which led her to actually demote herself after receiving a promotion thus going against our general societal conditioning that a promotion with more money is a good thing. Here's her story.

After many years working in various types of jobs and after her conversion to Buddhism, my friend started working for a concierge service. She was earning an hourly wage and working around 30 hours per week. After two years, she was offered a promotion, and a pretty significant raise, to manage the team of concierges in a building.

This meant managing a team of 10 people who needed to provide 24/7 coverage of concierge and security services. It was more responsibility—and as many of us have experienced when managing people, more headaches—because it meant dealing with employees' schedules, their sick days, their transportation issues, and anything else that meant they might not be able to show up for their shift. And as many of you in management know, if your employees can't show up and complete the objective, and you can't find anyone else to do it, you get to fill in to make sure the job gets done. For a 24/7 type of service, it means getting calls at any time with issues that must be dealt with immediately.

She took the position, was doing great in it, and everyone was happy with her work. Her clients adored her, her team respected her, and her management appreciated her. Everyone was happy—that is, except for her. The extra pay and prestige weren't worth the extra headache and responsibility. It was, quite frankly, messing with her chill.

So she quit.

She played her own game and chose flexibility and free time.

She asked for a demotion to go back to her original job and original salary, working 30 hours a week, and once she was off work, she was off. She wasn't receiving phone calls or dealing with schedules, shifts, or other issues that had been interrupting her free time.

Obviously, her manager tried to convince her to stay, but she knew what game she was playing—"Maximizing the Free Time"—and she chose her path accordingly. Instead of playing other people's games, where the rules would have directed her to accept more responsibility and more money, she played her own game and chose flexibility and free time.

The last time I saw her, she had married her significant other, had started a vegetable garden in her yard, and between income from work and Social Security, she was doing great financially. She was focused on meditating, on cooking and entertaining, on walking in the park, on sitting on her front porch, and on enjoying her stress-free free time.

She keeps score by the hours she's *not* at work or thinking about work and instead is doing the many other things she wants to do. Here's what her game looks like.

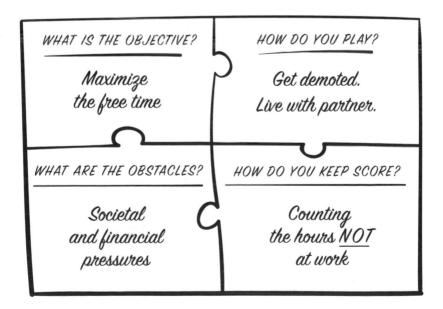

WHAT IS THE OBJECTIVE?	HOW DO YOU PLAY?
Maximize the free time	Get demoted. Live with partner.
WHAT ARE THE OBSTACLES?	HOW DO YOU KEEP SCORE?
Societal and financial pressures	Counting the hours NOT at work

The "Experience It All" Game

Another friend of mine is playing the "Experience It All" game. She is my most wacky rock-star friend. She's the person who lives life to its absolute fullest pretty much every minute of her day. She's the friend I call when I need to justify some (any) indulgence. She's the friend who will tell me to buy the shoes, buy the art, take the trip, upgrade to the suite, laugh out loud, and get wasted and make some bad decisions. I love her for it. She is a collector of things and experiences. She is really living her life.

She makes friends with people who work in cool stores all over the world. And they spontaneously send her things they think she'll like, including eclectic styles of shoes, handbags, clothes, and art. She takes trips and makes friends easily all over the world: Botswana, Australia, Cambodia, anywhere. She's one of the most alive people I know. She does bike races and triathlons and trekking adventures in exotic places.

Now. All of this "living life to the fullest" comes at a price. And people sometimes judge her as impulsive and compulsive and bad at managing money. After all, she's got massive credit card bills that go with these adventures and experiences, but she's fine with that. It's part of her game—like paying rent in Monopoly. She's bought enough life insurance to cover whatever debts her family members might be left with as a part of her estate. And she's assured them that if something takes her out early, her family will never have to mourn that "she never got to do XYZ," because she's done all of the XYZs she's ever wanted to do without hesitation.

Obviously she has to work. And most of the time, she's feisty at work and does a great job. But like all of us, some days she dreads going to the office. She dreads the people there. She dreads the drudgery and the load she is carrying. But she has to go to pay for all her cool stuff and cool experiences.

So she's decided to make going to work less painful by having all of her online shopping packages delivered to the office. This is for two reasons. First, nobody can steal packages off of her front porch, which has become a trend in her neighborhood; and second, it gives her an inspiring reason to get up and go to the office every day so she can pick up whatever new thing she ordered. And it works. Playing her own game keeps her motivated and happy enough at work to carry her through to the next adventure, the next trip, the next art purchase, or the next pair of shoes. Depending on your conditioning, this may sound superficial or irresponsible, but it's not. It's her choice. Instead of playing the game of holding it all in, of making herself small, of being conservative, of austerity as a way of preparing for the future. She's playing her game and she's doing what she needs to do in order to pay the bills. She's got it figured out in a way that works for her, and her game is to "Experience It All." And she's doing it.

Her scoreboard is the visual presence of all of the things around her that represent her experiences. This scoreboard includes the art, the fashion, the plane tickets, the furniture, and the photos. She's the one getting the most packages delivered to the office, and she's the one taking the most weekend getaways. Those are the symbols in her scoreboard that show her that she's winning her game.

Here's what her game looks like.

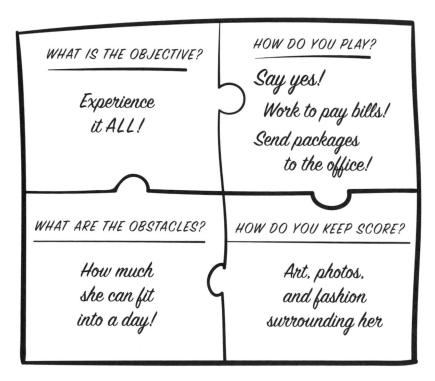

The "Build for the Next Generation" Game

Another friend of mine is playing the game of "Build for the Next Generation." He grew up in what could be described as one of the worst neighborhoods in a large city. Navigation services won't recommend driving through that neighborhood for safety reasons, and when he was growing up, many people close to him were impacted dramatically by various kinds of struggles. He wanted a better life for his family, so he got to work defining his own game.

After working as a trainer in a gym and selling insurance for a while, he started his own business in holistic health and training and started working especially with people with health issues. He has amassed an exclusive clientele and is positioning himself to expand into new areas. He engages with his clients on the mental, physical, and spiritual aspects of health, and he makes a positive impact on their lives.

Helping other people is also helping him with his own game. You see, he's doing all of this to make sure his daughters won't have to experience some of the things that he experienced as a young person. He is defining a new normal for them as a way to make sure they don't slide into bad situations, or as he says, "to keep them off the pole."

He moved outside of the city into a small town with a good public school. He rented a house with a yard, and he arranges his schedule so he can pick up his daughters after school every day. He supports the hell out of his wife, who is pursuing her PhD, and he has friends who help him stay focused on his big goals when the inevitable frustrations and obstacles arise.

He faces the challenges many of us face when we are trying not only to break even but also to amass wealth. He deals with the unexpected car repairs and the other things life throws at him, and he is determined to build something that he can leave to his daughters. He makes decisions every day in line with the game he has chosen to play, and he's going to win.

Here's what his game looks like.

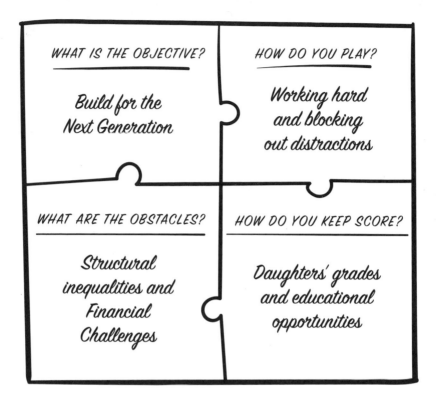

The "Creativity and Expression" Game

My next example is a friend who is incredibly creative in her thoughts and actions. She should be on stage or an artist or writing television comedies, but early in her life she had a child and needed a stable job and income as she was the sole provider. She started working in a stale corporate environment, but over the years, she has navigated her way into the most creative parts of that company, and she works in event marketing, with advertising agencies, and with sponsorships of concerts and festivals that are associated with her company's diversity and inclusion programs. As part of her job, she gets to go to biker festivals,

Latin music festivals, Pride parades, and a whole host of other activities where she gets to put on a uniform, talk to many different kinds of people, and let her creativity fly.

Being a single parent is not easy, and there were great external pressures for her to stay in an unhealthy relationship with her child's father. There were also pressures to deprioritize her own sources of joy and her creativity for the sake of her child. But instead of following those paths, she forged her own way, seeking and finding the right kinds of support from family members, friends, and community programs to make sure her daughter was taken care of while she worked, and she made sure to make creativity and fun a part of their daily life.

What I admire about her story is the way she figured out how to play her game even given some pretty serious responsibilities as a single mom. Just because you have responsibilities to someone else doesn't mean you have to give up your own game. And playing your own game doesn't mean you're being frivolous, irresponsible, or reckless with yourself or others. It just means that you are doing what *you* want to do and living according to *your* own objectives, as opposed to doing what you were conditioned to do.

Here's what her game looks like.

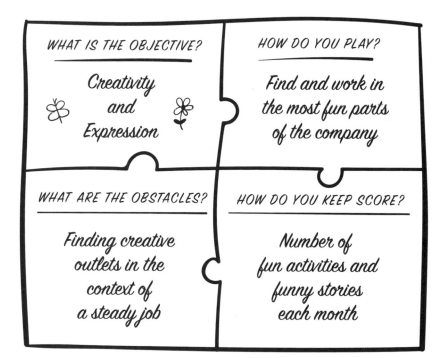

The "Create a Calm Environment" Game

In the years that I was a professor at a business school, I had a teaching assistant who, in retrospect, probably taught me more than I taught her. She was a Millennial, the kind that Boomers like to muse about. When she was 26, she married her high school sweetheart in a barn, and the ceremony was performed by one of their friends who got his marriage license online. Many of the themes of the wedding revolved around Harry Potter, and it was great and I loved every minute of it.

Professionally, she had worked in office environments and in healthcare clinics, had dealt with the stress of handling demanding students, and had thought about different options for getting her MBA or another type of master's degree to kick off an aggressive new career in healthcare or banking, which was expected of her given her family's focus on the traditional definition of success.

Then she paused and thought about her game. And instead of going to graduate school, she decided to open a small boutique to do facials and aesthetics instead. Choosing to go in this direction confused and frustrated some of her family members, and she had to manage the push back as their brains were having little freak-outs about her shift in direction.

Basically, she had decided that she didn't want to spend all day in an aggressive work environment, full of people who were being really competitive and stressing her out. She decided that she wanted to spend her days surrounded by people who were happy. Hence, a small boutique to focus on relaxation, enjoyment, and aesthetics. So while grading assignments for 500 MBA students at a top-tier university, she started to study and train for her new game.

I want to point out that she is still running a business and managing the stress that comes with that. But she's choosing what kind of business it is. She is choosing what kinds of stress she'll invite into her day and what kinds of stress she won't. She's choosing a kind of business where she opens the door in the morning and closes the door in the afternoon and leaves it behind instead of carrying it with her all the time. She's writing her own rules and playing her own game, prioritizing "calm" over a big title, a fancy office, and a big salary.

Her scoreboard is about her environment, how many people she made happy that day, and how she felt taking care of them in a symbiotic way. This is how she knows she's winning.

Here's what her game looks like.

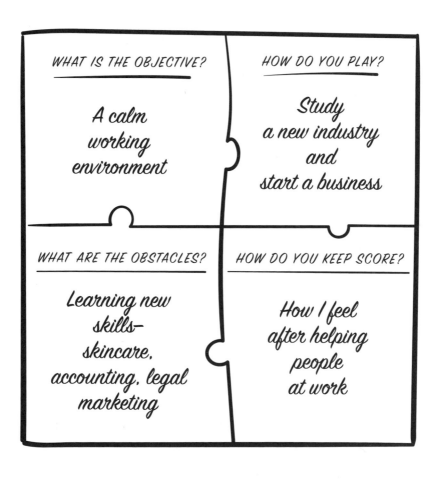

WHAT IS THE OBJECTIVE?	HOW DO YOU PLAY?
A calm working environment	Study a new industry and start a business
WHAT ARE THE OBSTACLES?	HOW DO YOU KEEP SCORE?
Learning new skills— skincare, accounting, legal marketing	How I feel after helping people at work

• • •

So when you're getting frustrated with something about your life, think about these examples and remember that lots of people are playing different games. Then remind yourself that you can play a different game too.

For fun someday, take a look at people around you and try to figure out what game they're playing. This really struck me one day when I was at a big aquarium on a weekday, and I attended a dolphin show with a friend and her child. There was a whole performance accompanying the show, with costumes and singing and dancing and diving. And in this performance, there was one guy who was singing and dancing his heart out. He was really enjoying what he was doing! And it occurred to me that this is what he does all day while I'm in an office on conference calls. So who's really winning? Answer: Maybe we both are winning because we are playing different games, but he definitely looked like he was enjoying performing much more than I have ever enjoyed being on a conference call.

I always look at people in airports and wonder what game they're playing. If you look closely, you can see it on people's faces. You can see the ones who are stressed out, and you know that they are a pawn in someone else's game. And then there are those of us who are happily passing through, on to our next destinations as part of our own bigger games.

Some people figure out their game early. They know from age five what they want to be when they grow up, and they do it. For the rest of us, we play someone else's game until we have enough life crises and finally we do the hard work to figure out our own game. My advice is to get it figured out early, and the earlier the better.

You Can Always Change Your Game

Remember, even though it may not feel like it sometimes, there are paths other than the one you feel like you should be on. There are other games to play. Start paying attention to what they might be and figure out which game is the one for you.

And don't forget that you can change your game. One game might work for a while, and then you may want to try another. *You* have the power to design and play your own game, and *you* have the power to change it if it no longer works for you. The important part is that it's *your* game—not the game that someone else is playing, or that someone else defines for you, or that is imposed on you one way or another.

You don't need to feel trapped or obligated to continue playing a game that you designed but that no longer works for you. Just go back and do the exercises in this book again and find your new game. There's no right or wrong way to live this one amazing life.

And know that over the course of your lifetime, you may change your game many times. And that's OK! The important part is that you are maintaining a level of clarity about what you want and that you're working toward it.

REMEMBER:

- There are many games you can play. It's your choice, so play the one you want to play!

CHAPTER 10

What Are You Waiting For?

I t may make you uncomfortable to admit, but you've been conditioned to play a certain game. And you may have conditioned others to play that game too.

It's difficult to step out of that conditioning, to see other options for ways to live your life, and to see different games that you can be playing. It takes awareness and courage and strength to design and play your own game instead of playing the one that others expect you to play. But it feels so good when you're doing it.

I want to leave you with some final perspectives that have helped me define my version of success and design my game. Hopefully they will be useful for you as you move forward in your own game.

Ditch the Timeline

When you're creating your game, first and foremost, ditch the timeline, whether it's imposed by you or by someone else. Measuring yourself against an externally imposed timeline is the best way to let life pass you by. Also, when you've set a timeline for yourself, whenever the unexpected happens and throws you off track—whether it's fun and surprise and opportunity or loss and struggle—you feel like a loser because you didn't hit a milestone by a specific date. Take the pressure off by removing the timeline.

This is really difficult for most people because we are taught to think in terms of timelines. Get a driver's license at 16, finish high school at 18, and finish college at 22. Then our timelines tell us by what age we should get a job and an apartment, buy a car, be in a serious relationship, get married, have kids, reach management and leadership levels at work, hit financial goals, buy a home, and do all of those other things we think we're supposed to be doing.

When I spoke with a colleague about this one day, she really freaked out. She said she couldn't even imagine a life game without a timeline and she asked me what that would even look like because it was so far-fetched for her. So I responded that it means that you know, no matter what age you are, you'll have opportunities to love and be loved in all sorts of ways by all sorts of people. (My experience is love rarely comes in the form I expect it to come in, but I have learned to embrace it none-theless.) It means you can get married in your 20s, 30s, 40s—or even your 80s. Some people get married once, some marry multiple times, and some not at all.

It means you can have kids over a range of 20–30 years of your adult life—or not at all. People have children through adoption, with a partner, or with the help of medical intervention. They can parent their children alone, with partners, and with extended support groups. And people who have become parents at various ages and under varying circumstances have led happy lives and have great kids, so the idea of an optimal age to have kids is an externally imposed one that you don't have to internalize or follow.

It means that you work on financial goals every single day and that living within your means is the best way to achieve them. As such, making decisions about renting versus buying a home or building a financial cushion aren't part of a timeline but rather part of your everyday job to take care of yourself—just like eating well, going to the gym, and sleeping.

It means finding work that fits into the rest of your life, working hard, and contributing to your organization. And knowing that if your work and value aren't being appreciated, or that your work situation just isn't fitting with the rest of what you want to be doing in your life, you can find another situation. Hitting a management or a VP level by a certain age is less important than contributing and being valued and having interesting work.

It can feel weird to let go of a timeline, but try it out. Let yourself be more expansive in your thinking and see where it gets you.

Focus on What Brings You Joy

Get focused on what brings you true joy—like petting your dog or feeling the wave rise up under your surfboard or creating something beautiful. Make sure your vision and plan include plenty of time for that.

Get focused on where you want to grow and have experiences—like learning a language or traveling to new places or learning to code or to cultivate a vegetable garden or dance or laugh or challenge yourself intellectually or at work with new assignments or writing a screenplay. These can be things that enhance your life both personally and professionally—because those two worlds actually go together in that the ways you want to grow personally also may help you grow professionally.

Get focused on where you want to grow and have experiences.

Then get focused on the kinds of people you want to do this with. Not specific names but qualities of people. Those who are supportive of you and who accept you for who you are and who will accompany you in your pursuit of joy and growth. Then go find more of these people and surround yourself with them!

People are playing different games, and remember that you can play a different game too.

And yes, we all have to pay our bills—so get focused on what that equation looks like too. But only after you've thought about where your joy comes from, what kinds of growth you are seeking, and what kinds of relationships you want to invite into your life. Fund those things first and then think about how big your house needs to be and what brands of clothes you want to buy.

Be Flexible

And yes—difficult things happen. It's part of life. So leave room for that and be kind to yourself. Take the pressure off yourself at work while you deal with health issues that arise. Know that everything will seem to stop for a year or two when an important relationship in your life ends abruptly from death or divorce. Know that your career will ebb and flow and not always move straight up, as companies grow and shrink and as industries appear and decline.

Give yourself the freedom and flexibility to continuously adapt, update, revise, and change your game. Like with a garden—you plant, things bloom, you prune, and things grow in new ways. Over and over. Include growth and also pruning and planting new kinds of flowers so that your game can grow and change to fit you. Avoid sticking rigidly to a game you designed but that no longer fits.

Don't Compare Yourself to Others

And finally . . . Don't compare yourself to others when you're trying to figure out if your life is going the way it needs to go. You're living your life. Other people are living theirs. Comparisons aren't valid because you're apples and they're oranges. You can both be awesome and both be winning your own games at the same time.

Instead, stay focused on what is right for you and let the external pressure to measure up to others fall away. It's harder than it sounds. But remember that your life is not about playing someone else's game, so don't measure

Stay focused on what is right for you and let the external pressure to measure up to others fall away.

yourself by their rules and standards of success. Design and play and win at your *own* game instead.

•   •   •

Stepping out of your current, known game to design and play your own, new game can feel scary. But isn't it scarier to live your life by someone else's rules? Isn't it scarier to play someone else's game your whole life instead of playing your own?

What are you waiting for?

Epilogue

As I've thought about playing my own game and about my responsibility to others, I have drawn on Khalil Gibran's book *The Prophet*, especially the chapter about children. He says that the role of a parent is to help a child become who they are supposed to be, not groom the child to be who the parent wants them to be. Basically, his point is that parents should help children design and play their own game, not insist that they play the parents' games. I take this philosophy to heart when I am with children, friends, colleagues, and family members, and I try to support them in becoming who they need to be. Gibran's thinking on this point is great advice in general.

I also think often about how, over time, I accumulated the baggage of other people's expectations, internalized it, and carried it around on my back for years and years and years. I have begun to visualize the conditioning process as others putting layers of expectations and assumptions on top of me, like layers and layers of clothing. I was covered in T-shirts and sweaters and jackets and coats and scarves and hats and backpacks of other people's expectations and assumptions to the point that I was physically, mentally, and emotionally weighed down by them.

My twenties and thirties were full of layers being added onto me at work, at school, and in relationships. Then the process of delayering began in my forties. I began shedding others' expectations and figuring out who I am and what I want without all those things that others had put on top of me.

I have slowly been shedding those layers, and each year I feel freer—and clearer—about what I want. Eventually, I imagine that I will be without the extra baggage, wearing just flip-flops and a sundress and wandering down a beach carefree.

I hope that after reading this book you will feel emboldened to go on your own journey of delayering from others' expectations and defining your own version of success. With courage, persistence, and support, I know you will be able to reach your own happy place where you will feel lighter and carefree. And I know you will be glad that you did.

Acknowledgments

The overwhelming emotion I have in my life is gratitude. I'm grateful for the people in my life. For those who have inspired me. For the opportunity to write this book. For the opportunity to share it with others.

I am particularly grateful to people who have helped me grow and who are there to cushion me when I fall down. These people include my mother and father, my sister, Carmelina, Any, Mopi, Naty, Mati, Pia, Feli, Syl, Dave, Shayne, Shelly, Lius, Meredita, Kris, Gret, Chris, Jessica, Quincy, Verne, Trang, Ines, Annice, and Leslie.

Also, I am grateful for the sources of inspiration life has brought to my doorstep including Steve Jobs's graduation speech about connecting the dots; Ai Wei Wei's work on challenging the status quo; Maya Angelou's short story "New Directions," reminding me I can always carve a new path if I want to; Anna Quindlen's *A Short Guide to a Happy Life*, reminding me to "Look at the view, young lady. Look at the view"; Natalie Merchant's song "Wonder," which reminds me "I'm a challenge to your balance"; and life's truly serendipitous interactions, like the day I was trying to make a major life decision and a man teaching his kid to ride a bike yelled out, "*Mirá adelante. Cuándo miras para atrás es cuando te caes*"—"Look forward! It's when you look backward that you fall down!" Indeed.

Many people helped make this book possible, including Iza, Cortnei, Lindsey, Jayme, Sandy, Sam, Elizabeth, Jen, Kim, Steve, Corrin, Justin, and more. Thank you for your guidance, input, expertise, and support.

Finally, I am grateful for the joy going forward that I trust life and the universe will bring. In fact, it has already begun. Who knew life could be so fun?

About the Author

Robin Moriarty, PhD, is a global business executive, professor, and writer who has lived on four continents and traveled to more than 60 countries. She has driven business initiatives that have had positive impacts on communities around the world, and she regularly shares her observations and advice on navigating complex work and life questions with students and professionals. She is fascinated by art, design, technology, human behavior, and basically whenever anyone challenges the status quo.